Beat Not Beat

*an anthology of California poets screwing
on the Beat and post-Beat tradition*

Beat Not Beat

*an anthology of California poets screwing
on the Beat and post-Beat tradition*

---

edited by
Rich Ferguson

co-edited by
S.A. Griffin, Alexis Rhone Fancher & Kim Shuck

~ 2022 ~

Beat Not Beat: an anthology of California poets screwing on the Beat and post-Beat tradition
© Copyright 2022 Moon Tide Press
All rights reserved. No part of this book may be used or reproduced in any manner whatsoever without written permission from either the publisher or the individual authors, except in the case of credited epigraphs or brief quotations embedded in articles or reviews.

Editor-in-chief
Eric Morago

Anthology Editor
Rich Ferguson

Anthology Associate Editors
S.A. Griffin, Alexis Rhone Fancher & Kim Shuck

Editor Emeritus
Michael Miller

Marketing & Media Director
Ellen Webre

Proofreader
Jim Hoggatt

Front cover art
Alexis Rhone Fancher

Book design
Michael Wada

Moon Tide logo design
Abraham Gomez

Beat Not Beat: an anthology of California poets screwing on the Beat and post-Beat tradition
is published by Moon Tide Press

Moon Tide Press
6709 Washington Ave. #9297
Whittier, CA 90608
www.moontidepress.com

FIRST EDITION

Printed in the United States

ISBN # 978-1-957799-04-9

CONTENTS

Foreword	12	*Rich Ferguson*
One Who is Always Arriving	15	Amy Gerstler
Invocation	16	Frank T. Rios
Would You Wear My Eyes?	17	Bob Kaufman
Path	18	Jack Hirschman
A Meditation on the Responsibility of the Poet	19	Allen J. Freedman
Calling 21st Century Poets	21	Dr. Mongo
The Tragedy Of The Leaves	25	Charles Bukowski
If You Are Going To Smoke	26	Jennifer Bradpiece
I Am 43 Still Stealing Cigarettes From My Mother	28	Luivette Resto
She Said Simile	29	Milo Martin
This Is	31	Amy Uyematsu
San Francisco Ocean Beach Blues	33	Devorah Major
Changing Light and Crows	34	Kim Shuck
The Dancer Steps Forward	35	Scott Wannberg
Dancing	38	Robert Hass
Don't Touch My Junk	42	D.A. Powell
The Beavers Have a Chat	43	Rick Lupert
Poetic Portraits	44	Carolyn Cassady
The Funny Style Cat	46	Saul White
I Never Have A Bad Day Except for the Ones That End in Y	47	Michael C Ford
Letter From Rosemary's Baby	48	MK Chavez
Desired by Ants	49	Gayle Brandeis
Promiscuous Girl and the Search for White Acceptance	50	Jessica M. Wilson
1999 to Mumia Abu-Jamal	52	Ronnie Burk
Creased Map of the Underworld	53	Kim Addonizio
You Should Only Give Head to Guys You Really Like	54	La Loca
The Kurosawa Champagne	58	Derrick Brown
When I Asked Him to Turn Me on He Said:	60	Alexis Rhone Fancher
God is an Asshole	61	Joe Pachinko
It Sucked Being a Teenager in the 80s	62	Annette Cruz

Man Claiming to be Tarzan Arrested Again	64	Charles Webb
Lullaby For an Imagined Child	65	Laurel Ann Bogen
Spring Swing	67	Tony Scibella
Venice by the Sea	68	Mike Sonksen
Mirrors are Sleeping Winds	71	Philomene Long
Flags	72	Peter Coyote
City on the Second Floor	74	Matt Sedillo
Annunciation at Pico and Sixth	75	Ron Koertge
Coyote in the Mission	76	Mary Tallmountain
Cosmopolitan Jungle	77	Kennon B. Raines
Dead Hours of Dawn	78	A.D. Winans
Progress	81	Linda J. Albertano
Returning	84	Gary Lemons
Movie Physics	85	Billy Burgos
Kamala Harris in Degrees Of Kevin Bacon	86	Suzi Kaplan Olmstead
Good Work, if You Can Get it	87	Bill Mohr
The Explanation of Pretty Much Everything	89	Paul Corman-Roberts
Then and Now	91	Ellaraine Lockie
She Said, "The Healing Meter Has Expired"	93	Susan Hayden
Fold	95	King Daddy
Unscheduled Poem	96	Brendan Constantine
Head Stop	97	Dennis Cruz
I Write and I Fuck	99	Yvonne De La Vega
White Trash Apocalypse	101	Pleasant Gehman
The Impossibility of an Anti-Banana Poem	103	Jimmy Jazz
Such A Heavenly Way to Die	104	Bucky Sinister
Mother Tongue	106	Tanya Ko Hong
He Really	107	Suzanne Lummis
Third Anniversary Poem from Neal to Carolyn	109	Neal Cassady
Poetic Guidance from Diane di Prima: A Found Poem*	110	Kitty Costello
We Know Monsters by Their Teeth	112	Kelly Grace Thomas
He Breathes	114	Diane di Prima
Poem For André Breton	116	Philip Lamantia
Anterior Speculation	117	Will Alexander

For The 'Feminist'	118	CLS Sandoval
Mary's Club	120	Jan Steckel
Palm	122	Natasha Dennerstein
3 Minutes	124	Richard Loranger
World News Brief	125	Ken Wainio
Vaccine	126	Marc Olmsted
Duplicitous Unconditional	127	Danny Baker
Jails Have Atm Machines Now	132	Cassandra Dallett
Sankofa Scars	135	A.K. Toney
A Supermarket In California	137	Clint Margrave
Dystopian Revenge For The New Year Hell Of It	139	Mike M Mollett
Tendencies	140	Julie Rogers
Transient	141	Terry Wolverton
Fox	142	Kenneth Rexroth
If Someone Paints A Plant, Are They Objectifying It?	143	Nicelle Davis
The Iceberg Theory	145	Gerald Locklin
Life Is A Dream	146	Aram Saroyan
Glory To The Heroes	147	S.A. Griffin
The Wedding Of Everything	148	Bob Flanagan
Destruction	150	Joanne Kyger
Another Exercise In Love	151	Dorianne Laux
The Transforming Ways	152	Eric Brown
Stella On Friday	154	Pam Ward
Famous Poets In The Sack	156	Briana Muñoz
A Kara: U Kara: M Kara: Iti	157	Peggy Dobreer
Temporal Beatitudes	158	Kimi Sugioka
Defense Offense Back Fence	160	Q.R. Hand Jr.
Instruments Of Deconstruction	162	Henry Mortensen
Black Lives	165	Nikki Blak
Counting, On New Year's Morning, What Powers Yet Remain To Me	167	Jane Hirshfield
Death To The Real World	168	G. Murray Thomas
California Orange Light Sutra	171	Lee Rossi
Ode To Iron	173	Elisabeth Adwin Edwards
Beautiful	174	Jeremy Radin
Skull Cave	175	Clive Matson
Root	176	Kathryn De Lancellotti
An Afternoon Painting	178	Bob Branaman
Tempus Fugit	179	E.K. Keith
When brown bodies make the news	181	Aruni Wijesinghe

Social Distance	183	Kevin Ridgeway
Feral Like Me	185	Iris Berry
But of Life	188	Kenneth Patchen
Dry Water	189	Jim Morrison
Exquisite Corpses	190	Johnette Napolitano
When Called in for Questioning	191	Rich Ferguson
With Coltrane on the Great Western Divide	192	John Brantingham
The Rarest of Sightings	194	Conney Williams
For the Birds: A Charm of Goldfinches	196	Cecilia Woloch
We're Far Below the Dark Shroud Nights	197	Daniel Yaryan
Le Soleil & La Lune	199	Laure-Anne Bosselaar
The Small Country	200	Ellen Bass
On the Desert Wind this Morning	201	A. Razor
Peacock	204	Dion O'reilly
For Poets in Autumn	206	Holly Prado
Tulips Unbound	207	Jamie Asaye Fitzgerald
The Inverse History of Spilled Mouth	208	Kelly Gray
Poetry is a Prayer	210	Harry E. Northup
Will the Poets Keep Quiet?	211	Judith Ayn Bernhard
The Voice of the River	212	Lewis Macadams
Song of the Turkey Buzzard	214	Lew Welch
Jack's Advice	218	RD Armstrong
I am a Poet	219	Jack Micheline
Goals	222	Jessica Loos
Untitled	223	Stuart Z. Perkoff
O Soul Concealed Below	225	Wanda Coleman
Headnote to a Done Poem	227	Douglas Kearney
Perhaps	231	Luis J. Rodriguez
A Love Poem and a Poem of Thanks and Memory ao My Wife	233	Steve Abee
Night Song of the Los Angeles Basin	234	Gary Snyder
Even Birds are Complicated	236	Phoebe Macadams

A (Prose)Poem Strictly for the Local Scene, Like, Maybe it's an Open Letter to Herbert Q. Caen	237	William J. Margolis
The Earth and the Stars in the Palm of our Hand	240	Fred Voss
They Feed they Lion	243	Philip Levine
The Ways of Remembering Women	244	Lynne Thompson
The Unnamed Garden	247	Luke Johnson
Song of the Broken Dice	249	Sarah Maclay
Moon Skin	251	K.R. Morrison
21st Century Death Poem	252	Chris Tannahill
In the Sea of Dolphins, I am a Manta Ray	254	Don Kingfisher Campbell
I Was Born Between Two Waves	255	Majid Naficy
Proposal	256	James Cagney
One Day	257	Joseph Millar
Shot	258	Nelson Gary
A New World in our Hearts	259	Richard Modiano
Sky Throwing Bullets of Hail	261	Jerry The Priest
Doing Nothing	262	Kim Dower
At the Studio	264	Mariano Zaro
The Reading was a Benefit	266	Linda Noel
On the Road Before Rain	268	Stephen Meadows
Breath	269	Terry Adams
North Beach	271	Harold Norse
A Sketch About Genocide	273	Tongo Eisen-Martin
Smolder	275	Eric Morago
Our Son Comes Over	277	David L. Ulin
Chalcedony	279	Amélie Frank
Prayer for the Season	280	Christine No
Can't You Hear the Wind Howl?	282	Frank X. Gaspar
The Smog's Vibrant Gown	283	Kevin Opstedal
September 24th, Waiting at the Bart Station Ahead of Yet Another Climate Strike	284	Greer Nakadegawa-Lee
Crossing Over (Exhibit #204)	285	Larry Colker
Alley-House Thinking	286	Ann Menebroker
Matrilineage	287	Sylvia Ross
An Exercise in Love	288	Michelle Bitting

"The Last <<True>> Yugoslav"	290	Charlie Getter
This is Wilmington	292	Jack Brewer
Branded	294	Tate Swindell
"Buk Rhymes With Puke," Charles Bukowski Said to the Lady at The Liquor Store in the 1973 Taylor Hackford Documentary Bukowski	296	Joan Jobe Smith Voss
Lunches with Linda	298	Soheyl Dahi
For Ukraine	299	Neeli Cherkovski
Salute!	302	Lawrence Ferlinghetti
2016: The Year whe 20th Century Finally Died	304	Ellyn Maybe
Apology to Greta Thunberg	306	Doug Knott
Let's Voyage into the New American House	309	Richard Brautigan
Re: 2016	310	David Meltzer
Call	311	francEyE
Afterword	*312*	
About The Authors	*314*	
Acknowledgements	*353*	

Art is love is God

—Wallace Berman

FOREWORD

When I was selected by the National Beat Poetry Foundation, Inc. (NBPF) to serve as the State of California Beat Poet Laureate during the outset of the Covid pandemic in 2020, my reactions were many. No doubt, I was highly honored to receive such an award, but I also realized many of my poetry peers were equally deserving of such an honor. Therefore, it became even more important to share this award in whatever ways possible: provide spaces for lesser-known and marginalized poets to share their work; offer community outreach and educational services; create new possibilities for artists in different mediums to collaborate. Unfortunately, the Covid quarantine limited my ability to accomplish these goals.

Still, I did my best to connect with poets worldwide, engaging in various collaborations with musicians, visual artists, and other poets. I judged poetry contests, emceed and performed in various Zoom events, hosted the rare live event, and blurbed fellow poets' collections. However, whatever I did, I wanted to do still more. It wasn't until a conversation with one of my collaborators—the poet and visual artist Kathleen Florence—that the idea of this anthology came into being. Kathleen helped me realize that since I couldn't get out into the world to celebrate with my fellow California poets, I should bring them together for a celebration within these pages.

Receiving this award has also made me consider what it means to be a "Beat" poet. Over the years, I've been inspired by the wisdoms and wordplay of seminal Beat poets like Bob Kaufman, Allen Ginsberg, Diane di Prima, and the like. Their utilization of inventive language, their exploration of engaging themes (politics, spirituality, and social issues), and dynamic presentation in live settings have fueled my writing and performance. Still, these poets are not my only inspiration. As with all poets (Beat, not-Beat, etc.), there are many flavors blended into our work's creation. My music background, for one, has been a huge inspiration. My drumming has influenced my sense of rhythm and musicality when creating, editing, and performing my work. This musicality is one of the many flavors contained within certain poets I admire: Patti Smith, Kamau Daáood, and Saul Williams to name a few.

I was first introduced to Beat poetry back in the 80s. Upon graduating from Rutgers University, I promptly packed up my drums, stereo, clothes into my Toyota and made a beeline for San Francisco. My first stop: City Lights Bookstore. I was immediately drawn to a copy of Gregory Corson's *Gasoline*. I was in awe of his mindbomb ability to blow one's mind through Shelleyesque and streetwise lyrical inventiveness. From then on, I was hooked. I began reading Ferlinghetti and Denise Levertov. I regularly carried Gary Snyder's *Turtle Island* and Philip Lamantia's *Becoming Visible* in my bag. I started reading my own poetry all around town: from North Beach to Fort Mason, the Lower Haight to the East Bay. I had the good fortune to be mentored by various members of the poetry community. These guardian angels of the poetic vanguard helped me hone my craft and voice as I grew up on stage.

It was during this time I first witnessed Anne Waldman perform poetry. I'd heard many amazing things about her but never really *got it* until seeing her live. She prowled the stage like a panther; her body, mind, and spirit were connected to otherworldly electricity. She also performed her work by memory. This was a transformative moment for me. I began memorizing my work to better embody the verbal moods and rhythms I was creating. I, too, wanted to cultivate and honor that kind of rebellious, creative energy I'd witnessed in Waldman's work.

This sense of artistic vitality was also alive and well throughout the 80s San Francisco music and arts scene. From folk to punk, from dance to spontaneous street performers, we rebelled in some form or another in the shadows of Reaganomics. Like the Beats and post-Beats, we were tuned into societal and political matters, rejected economic materialism, continually worked to hone our voices in more conscious and engaging ways.

Upon moving to L.A. in the early 90s, I was blessed to fall into an equally inspiring poetry and artistic community. It was then I first saw S.A. Griffin perform with the Carma Bums. Their work not only embodied many of the hallmarks of the Beat/post-Beat tradition I'd experienced in San Francisco, but the Carma Bums further cemented the idea of how poetry could be transformed into inventive and rebellious Dada'esque presentations. After that, I began attending and performing events throughout the city, from the World Stage in Leimert Park to Beyond Baroque in Venice, throughout Silver Lake, Echo Park, downtown, and East L.A. It's through these experiences and more that I've witnessed some of the finest poets this city has to offer. And while their themes, content, and delivery styles may vary, all contain energy, electricity, and a sense of musicality in their words and live performances.

To curate this collection, I relied upon the editorial assistance of Kim Shuck (former Poet Laureate of S.F.), Alexis Rhone Fancher (poet, photographer, and editor at Cultural Daily), and S.A. Griffin (longtime poet/performer and editor of the Outlaw Bible of American Poetry). I knew they'd be able to stretch my abilities as a poet and editor. They have done that and more: they have introduced me to young, older, and marginalized voices. Poets whose work is vibrant, courageous, wise, and wise-cracking. Unique and dynamic voices discussing social, political, sexual, and gender issues in lyrical, musical, and inventive ways.

This by no means is a definitive collection of Beat, post-Beat, or poets that fall into the gray areas in between these categories. It is, however, my attempt to honor many California poets that have inspired my writing and performance through the years.

While some of the original Beats have said that the Beat movement was a certain period in their writing lives and that they went on to create many other forms of poetry, the echoes of the Beat movement have no doubt left their mark on the poetic tradition. Be it through rap, rhythm, humor, issues of politics, sexuality, social justice, and gender equality, the poetry community continues to flourish. I wish I had the time and funds to create a more extensive collection; to allow the space to celebrate far more California poets. That will perhaps come later. Until then, let the beat go on…

Rich Ferguson
June, 2022

Amy Gerstler

ONE WHO IS ALWAYS ARRIVING

You arrive as a limping bird who can still fly.

You arrive as an inscribed leaf I need to read.

Amid morning uproar, you arrive, riven

yet complete. You arrive at night as admonition,

as apples striving for ripeness in their bowl,

as herds lapping at a watering hole, as a torrent

of warnings and blessings, as a stream of belief

so molton that the joys, grudges and griefs

your arrivals inspire require infinite disguises.

Frank T. Rios

INVOCATION

dear lady
my hands hang
like ghosts
in sunlight

& what there is to say
the sharing of a clumsy act
of something else pulled
from the blistered page

burns fields
melts steel
makes man extend
his shovel into the flame
feel more color
turn to rubber

can't stand over it long
thinks dust against bone

a machine dream lingering
long after he turns to home

forgetting why it all happens
just this way

& as a face
to recognize
her love
responsible

receives the poem
as one rides
unbroken
to confession.

Bob Kaufman

WOULD YOU WEAR MY EYES?

My body is a torn mattress,
Disheveled throbbing place
For the comings and goings
Of loveless transients.
The whole of me
Is an unfurnished room
Filled with dank breath
Escaping in gasps to nowhere.
Before completely objective mirrors
I have shot myself with my eyes,
But death refused my advances.
I have walked on my walls each night
Through strange landscapes in my head.
I have brushed my teeth with orange peel,
Iced with cold blood from the dripping faucets.
My face is covered with maps of dead nations;
My hair is littered with drying ragweed.
Bitter raisins drip haphazardly from my nostrils
While schools of glowing minnows swim from my mouth.
The nipples of my breasts are sun-browned cockleburrs;
Long-forgotten Indian tribes fight battles on my chest
Unaware of the sunken ships rotting in my stomach.
My legs are charred remains of burned cypress trees;
My feet are covered with moss from bayous, flowing across my floor.
I can't go out anymore.
I shall sit on my ceiling.
Would you wear my eyes?

Jack Hirschman

PATH

Go to your broken heart.
If you think you don't have one, get one.
To get one, be sincere.
Learn sincerity of intent by letting
life enter because you're helpless, really,
to do otherwise.
Even as you try escaping, let it take you
and tear you open
like a letter sent
like a sentence inside
you've waited for all your life
though you've committed nothing.
Let it send you up.
Let it break you, heart.
Broken-heartedness is the beginning
of all real reception.
The ear of humility hears beyond the gates.
See the gates opening.
Feel your hands going akimbo on your hips,
your mouth opening like a womb
giving birth to your voice for the first time.
Go singing whirling into the glory
of being ecstatically simple.
Write the poem.

Allen J. Freedman

A MEDITATION ON THE RESPONSIBILITY OF THE POET

let us assume
for just one moment
that our poetry does matter

not in some aesthetic sense
in which of course it does
like every other art
possess its proper form
and substance
but as matter in the world
possessing weight and moment
so that it does move
not merely to some pleasant
or unpleasant action

let us assume
that we are poets
fellows of an ancient order

> *beneficial*
> *dangerous*
> *significant*

that we possess our craft in measure
that our craft possesses us
that we must be responsible
for every word we speak
and that our words retain their power
even when the ink and paper
have been lost

let us assume all this
for just one moment
then examine where

and how we may be led
in disposition of our power
and the crafting of our poems

Dr. Mongo

CALLING 21ST CENTURY POETS
(First Call)

Calling 21st Century Poets,
Hardcore/vitriolic/underground Poets,
Outspoken/spoken word/guerilla Poets
to challenge the system –
declare war on class and privilege,
homelessness…. poverty/hunger;
hoist the flag, light the torch
of love and peace;
burn pyramid pyres and set the world aflame
with scorching truth.

Calling 21st Century Poets…
to confront/tear down/pulverize
stone-age myths/lore/superstitions
and the reign of recycled/refrigerated
hypocrisy/falsehood
and questionable paradigms…

Calling 21st Century Poets…
underground/guerilla Poets,
outspoken/spoken word Poets
to deliver fiery words,
constant tirades, harsh verbal assaults,
oratorical deathblows against
tyranny/intimidation
torture/execution, blanket assassinations
and forced suicides –

    21st Century Poets against
injustice/racism/sexism
prejudice/bigotry, ethnic cleansing
and border vigilantism
steeped in opinionated ologies/isms;

21st Century Poets against
executive/legislative/judicial exclusion/
slavery/genocide/extinction;
21st Century Poets against
pseudo-historians/preachers
personalizing hatred, race supremacy
and fanning incendiary flames of fanaticism
coded in the written and spoken word

Calling to arms 21st Century Poets
dissident/revolutionary lip masters
to hurl explosive word bombs
at corrupt, self-serving institutions,
producers of dumb down mentalities
to serve and protect the pompous,
loquacious, theo-philosophical gurus and
eccentric social planners,
Intellectualizing from swelled heads
squeezed by helmets, stocking caps
and greasy do-rags; cloaking their frail,
twisted bodies beneath white frocks, robes,
camouflaged khakis and three-pieced suits...

Calling 21st Century Poets
to stand/step up and revive the voices
of Ezekiel/Jeremiah
and prophets howling in the wilderness;
throating denunciatory complaint/protest
against eroders of freedom and liberty;
poisoners of ecosystems/environment,
village/community, mind/body
with stealth flying salt shakers
dispensing germ/disease/plague
on unsuspecting mothers/fathers/
sons/daughters and live-in pets...

Calling 21st Century Poets...
to rail against government-sponsored
drug prohibition, agricultural arsonists' –
armed global Juggernauts –
financed by the military-industrial complex,
carrying out scorched earth policies
with search and destroy brutality
in our backyards and homes...

Calling dedicated/frontline/uncorruptible Poets
outspoken/spoken word Poets
to expose the pharmaceutical-government-
university-complex; the privatized-prison-
criminal justice system complex;
21st Century Poets to unmask
zebrine provocateurs
spewing hatred/discord from spaceships
and cavernous catacombs...

Calling all 21st Century Poets,
hardcore/vitriolic/underground Poets,
outspoken/spoken word, guerilla Poets,
iconoclastic/revolutionary/diehard Poets
to pound home Milton's dictum:
(The poem is mightier than the sword.)
And do battle against powerful, greedy
corporate musketeers, plutocrats,
oligarchs, international bankers and
unprincipled industrialists
shipping deadly viruses, contaminated foods
and weapons to impoverished Third World nations;
flooding markets with cloned, vegetative
and meat products approved by underhanded
USDA inspectors; neatly wrapped and packaged
at fast food chains, tempting our finger-licking-
good-appetites with assembly-line biscuits
and bleached French fries...

Calling 21st Century Poets..
verbal soldiers, oral mercenaries/crusaders,
David-versus-Goliath types
to slingshot vituperative diatribes,
wielding oxgoads and donkey jawbones
as did Shamgar and Samson;
to crumble pillars of corruption
erected on propagandized foundations
footing ignorance and fear;
expose and rebuke appointed turncoats
sitting in high places and overseeing
governments while usurping and compromising
civil individual rights...

Calling 21 Century Poets
to raise up a hibernating/narcotized people,
a complacent/forgetful/gullible people,
a trusting/loving/rainbow people
to raise the bar and lambaste/admonish/censure
and condemn poachers and polluters
killing and testing death-concoctions
on indigenous/aboriginal/poor/oppressed
conquered/imprisoned cargo
snatched and shipped from past tense
to present day penitentiaries –
'business as usual' concentration camps,
black and brown leper colonies dotting
rural landscapes with oversized pill-boxes
controlled and operated by chameleonic devils.

Calling... calling.... calling... 21st Century Writers/
Musicians/Rappers/Activists/Citizens/Poets
of the world to speak out
against capital punishment IS MURDER
against manufactured starvation (food not bombs)
against flagrant child labor/deforestation
international espionage/global/domestic terrorism
and weapons of mass destruction...

Calling 21st Century Poets to examine
and question policies of:

WTO, IMF, WB, FCC, IBM, FBI, CIA, DAR, LAPD, NYPD,
GOP, IRS, ATMs, FHA, DEA, IRS, INS...

This poet has just begun.

Charles Bukowski

THE TRAGEDY OF THE LEAVES

I awakened to dryness and the ferns were dead,
the potted plants yellow as corn;
my woman was gone
and the empty bottles like bled corpses
surrounded me with their uselessness;
the sun was still good, though,
and my landlady's note cracked in fine and
undemanding yellowness; what was needed now
was a good comedian, ancient style, a jester
with jokes upon absurd pain; pain is absurd
because it exists, nothing more;
I shaved carefully with an old razor
the man who had once been young and
said to have genius; but
that's the tragedy of the leaves,
the dead ferns, the dead plants;
and I walked into the dark hall
where the landlady stood
execrating and final,
sending me to hell,
waving her fat, sweaty arms
and screaming
screaming for rent
because the world had failed us
both.

Jennifer Bradpiece

IF YOU ARE GOING TO SMOKE

Smoke naked drinking Mezcal
as often as possible.
Preferably in a light warm rain.

Smoke in a disheveled bed
of orgasmed friends
or lone strangers.

Smoke because it is so beautifully
painful to talk to another human.

Smoke because you think
you are going to break apart.

Smoke because the singeing paper cylinder
allows the breath between some space;
allows the soft trade of unseen
weights as balanced water.

Smoke because you are almost safe
on that burning buoy, that ember anchor,
that ashen rope.

Smoke because it focuses you entirely.

Smoke while glistening
from moving music beyond song
through your bones
for hours in a broken body.

Smoke because it makes waiting in line bearable.
Makes tiny exit ramps
on tumultuous flights of social gathering.

Smoke exultant when tears flow
or during storms of anger.

Smoke because it ties tight to your skin
every moment you must remember.

(But if you don't smoke, don't smoke.
What you don't know can't kill you.)

Smoke when words pour straight
from vein to pen, or rain
on keyboards through fingertips.
Ignite the stick when the words hide
and they will call out to you.

Smoke singing, "you made me forget myself…"

Smoke when breathing
inside your body
is the smoldering aftermath
of bombs exploding every instant.

Smoke because no one questions
whether lighting a cigarette
is the most sane thing
a soldier can do in times of war.

Smoke because you smoked with
someone you love
and they are no longer here.

Luivette Resto

I AM 43 STILL STEALING CIGARETTES FROM MY MOTHER

Two decades since my first drag
I find myself stealing cigarettes from my mother's stash,
held in the top left-hand kitchen drawer.

She doesn't count them like I did in college
when loosies could be bought without getting one killed
they were expensive even back then
when I was known for throwing lit cigarettes at people
particularly men with their inane conversation starters.

Growing up with a chain smoker I vowed my disgust
the Newport menthol smell attached to my Catholic school uniform,
overpowering the Aquanet in my bun.

My abuelo looked down on smokers
so naturally all of the women in my family
smoked out back, when he was asleep, or working late nights at the
bodega the same place where they would buy cigarettes.

They didn't want any part of Pedro's wrath
Las mujeres decentes no fuman.
Smoking was for whores, women with low morals,
women who fought on command.

Inhaling the nicotine
outside of my mother's house
I think about the first time I gave a man a blowjob,
allowed a man to put his hands on me,
watched my mother show me how to fight.

Perhaps Pedro was right,
as I squash the cigarette butt
back and forth with the heel of my shoe.

Milo Martin

SHE SAID SIMILE

She said it's like falling asleep in the snow
like your bathwater growing slowly cold

She said it's like holding scissors against the soft part of your inner arm
like watching a medieval barn fall into decay

She said it's like following an ambulance deep into the suburbs
like kneeling alone in a cathedral listening to candles

She said it's like putting your coat on getting ready to leave
like witnessing the runt of the litter struggle for a teat

She said it's like being so young before the war
like learning not to talk to people you shouldn't

She said it's like combing the hair of a balding man
like coming home to find your goldfish on the floor

She said it's like tripping in a three-legged picnic race
like having to phone information for your own number

She said it's like dead leaves folding under the mud and the broken glass
like climbing seven flights of stairs to a soiree gone bad

She said it's like waking up and not knowing where you are sometimes
like not owning a ticket for where you want to go

She said it's like deer who've lost their footing in the forest inferno
like geese blown off course by the merciless winter wind

She said it's like your axle coming unhinged around a tight corner
like singing for your supper to the Ethiopian night

She said it's like, it's like, it's like a simile without a corresponding image
like a DeMaupassant story with the last page torn out

She said it's like blowing smoke rings with your eyes closed
like rings of smoke slipping through the seals of your eyes

She said it's like finishing your last cigarette
and putting it out with the toe of your boot

She said it's like, she said it's like,
she said it's like, THAT...

Amy Uyematsu

THIS IS

karma / what goes around vs. how could this happen in america/ how deplorable/ unbelievable /

NO, how inevitable / white supremacists and fascists storming the capitol building / brandishing

nooses and the confederate flag / haven't we seen this before / ask any native tribal survivor / ask

the thousands whose father or mother or child was lynched / the millions who witnessed the smug

white cop pressing his knee on george floyd's neck / imagine a young black or latino mugging

for cameras with his feet on nancy pelosi's desk / we all know he'd never get the chance / no

black lives matters protestors in the mob / we saw the t-shirts proclaiming 'camp auschwitz'

and 'six million are not enough' / remember charlottesville / trump telling us there were very fine

people among those who marched with torches and nazi slogans / and now he comforts his darling

capitol terrorists / the insurrection still going on / he understands their pain and loves them /

THIS IS the america people of color have always known / the so-called democracy that forced us

into reservations, plantations, world war ii concentration camps, border detention jails / the glorious land-of-the-free where malcolm predicted the chickens would come home to roost / THIS IS who

we are

devorah major

SAN FRANCISCO OCEAN BEACH BLUES

i hear its sough and sigh as it washes refuse onto the shore
        more frequently than the shells I used to capture
                or the smooth stones
                          i used to pick up
and finger
before warming them in my palms
        then returning each
                back to the shore's damp edge
i want its
      ancient ocean scent to sidle into my nostrils
           the moist kelp vines beginning to dry, to rot
                    gull emptied tiny crab carcasses
i thirst for the salt that envelops the air
        lingers on the edges of my lashes
i yearn for the beach spume-rich and noisy
        before its sand was turned matte black
                    & steel gray, hiding
    its soft tan skin beneath smelted oil
its foam skirts full of trash
        dying fish and marooned whales

we need
to steer our sturdy ships to the garbage patch of plastic scum
              hovering between hawaii and california   and
fill those
        vessels' holds with our putrid waste
return it to its source

so the ocean
can continue to sing a hymn for her children growing in deep sea
forests

Kim Shuck

CHANGING LIGHT AND CROWS

Today we are the streaked and
Fallen leaves in the red light of
Bookstore and bar in the tumble of
Road works and at least one
Tree full of crows and
Five-fingered leaves the
Stroking wind and the
Purposeful fog in these moments
Before the walk down a
Main street through an
Idea of history that is
Stretched until smooth
Drawn between at least two people but
Usually more this is a song too this
Dangerous need to rewrite and we the
Leaves blow and skitter and
Know a different truth

Scott Wannberg

THE DANCER STEPS FORWARD

The dancer stays home
digging in his earth, looking for the bone that will
sing to him.

His friends have run off to Europe.
They groan, pull their hair, wail,
America is a paltry place for the imagination.
They hit the walls, deny their past.
They become good Europeans.

The dancer shrugs in his New Jersey afternoon,
begins to dance
around the circumference of his native ground.
I've got to learn the language, he says.
I've got to follow through on the syntax.
There is a music here. Don't be so quick to deny it.

He steps out onto the American earth.
People come to him, ask,
Do you know what they are doing across the sea?
They are writing epics!
They are tearing up the linear fabric.

Let me do my digging, he says.
And the music that is alive there
begins to attach itself to his skin
in that hard-working New Jersey afternoon.
His patients come, his patients go.
The good doctor knows there is a music
here.

One of his good friends,
an old schoolboy pal
who will later do time for mixing aesthetics and politics,
keeps haranguing him to come to Europe.
I'm too busy digging, he says, there is a music here, I tell you,
and my job is to find it,
learn it,
sing it.

You can have your poets of Provence,
you can have Confucius.
I'm hunting a different game altogether.
The sun grows hot.
He begins to sweat there in the yard,
digging.

He takes a drink of water.
We leave him at his work
as night quietly shows up.
Later he steps onto the front porch.
He will begin naming the new rhythm,
the kind of rhythm that you recognize
on the street, maybe.

Not some secret arcane language,
not some language you need a dictionary to understand,
the kind of rhythm
you can maybe
figure out all by yourself
as you roll it around in your mouth,
as you begin to say it and it begins to sing you.

There is a music in the American idiom, he says,
and wipes his face for the last time,
and begins to think about going up to bed.
Tomorrow is another song.
Tomorrow will be other patients and
words to discover and stories behind such words
that illuminate.

The game, after all,
is one of discovery.
The day you stop finding out things
is the day
you might as well
turn yourself in for good.

He slowly makes his way upstairs to
his beloved Flossie.
There is a music here.
All you have to do is believe,
and the rest
is just
some history of
song
and love.

Robert Hass

DANCING

The radio clicks on—it's poor swollen America,
Up already and busy selling the exhausting obligation
Of happiness while intermittently debating whether or not
A man who kills fifty people in five minutes
With an automatic weapon he has bought for the purpose
Is mentally ill. Or a terrorist. Or if terrorists
Are mentally ill. Because if killing large numbers of people
With sophisticated weapons is a sign of sickness—
You might want to begin with fire, our early ancestors
Drawn to the warmth of it—from lightning,
Must have been, the great booming flashes of it
From the sky, the tree shriveled and sizzling,
Must have been, an awful power, the odor
Of ozone a god's breath; or grass fires,
The wind whipping them, the animals stampeding,
Furious, driving hard on their haunches from the terror
Of it, so that to fashion some campfire of burning wood,
Old logs, must have felt like feeding on the crumbs
Of the god's power and they would tell the story
Of Prometheus the thief, and the eagle that feasted
On his liver, told it around a campfire, must have been,
And then—centuries, millennia—some tribe
Of meticulous gatherers, some medicine woman,
Or craftsman of metal discovered some sands that,
Tossed into the fire, burned blue or flared green,
So simple the children could do it, must have been,
Or some soft stone rubbed to a powder that tossed
Into the fire gave off a white phosphorescent glow.
The word for chemistry from a Greek—some say Arabic—
Stem associated with metal work. But it was in China
Two thousand years ago that fireworks were invented—
Fire and mineral in a confined space to produce power—
They knew already about the power of fire and water
And the power of steam: 100 BC, Julius Caesar's day.
In Alexandria, a Greek mathematician produced
A steam-powered turbine engine. Contain, explode.
"The earliest depiction of a gunpowder weapon

Is the illustration of a fire-lance on a mid-12th-century
Silk banner from Dunhuang." Silk and the silk road.
First Arab guns in the early fourteenth century. The English
Used cannons and a siege gun at Calais in 1346.
Cerigna, 1503: the first battle won by the power of rifles
When Spanish "arquebusiers" cut down Swiss pikemen
And French cavalry in a battle in southern Italy.
(Explosions of blood and smoke, lead balls tearing open
The flesh of horses and young men, peasants mostly,
Farm boys recruited to the armies of their feudal overlords.)
How did guns come to North America? 2014,
A headline: DIVERS DISCOVER THE SANTA MARIA
One of the ship's Lombard cannons may have been stolen
By salvage pirates off the Haitian reef where it had sunk.
And Cortes took Mexico with 600 men, 17 horses, 12 cannons.
And LaSalle, 1679, constructed a seven-cannon barque,
Le Griffon, and fired his cannons upon first entering the
     continent's
Interior. The sky darkened by the terror of the birds.
In the dream time, they are still rising, swarming,
Darkening the sky, the chorus of their cries sharpening
As the echo of that first astounding explosion shimmers
On the waters, the crew blinking at the wind of their wings.
Springfield Arsenal, 1777. Rock Island Arsenal, 1862.
The original Henry rifle: a sixteen shot .44 caliber rimfire
Lever-action, breech-loading rifle patented—it was an age
Of tinkerers—by one Benjamin Tyler Henry in 1860,
Just in time for the Civil War. Confederate casualties
In battle: about 95,000. Union casualties in battle:
About 110,000. Contain, explode. They were throwing
Sand into the fire, a blue flare, an incandescent green.
The Maxim machine gun, 1914, 400-600 small caliber rounds
Per minute. The deaths in combat, all sides, 1914-1918
Was 8,042,189. Someone was counting. Must have been.
They could send things whistling into the air by boiling water.
The children around the fire must have shrieked with delight
1920: Iraq, the peoples of that place were "restive,"
Under British rule and the young Winston Churchill
Invented the new policy of "aerial policing," which amounted,
Sources say, to bombing civilians and then pacifying them
With ground troops. Which led to the tactic of terrorizing

             civilian
Populations in World War II. Total casualties in that war,
Worldwide: soldiers, 21 million; civilians, 27 million.
They were throwing sand into the fire. The ancestor who stole
Lightning from the sky had his guts eaten by an eagle.
Spread-eagled on a rock, the great bird feasting.
They are wondering if he is a terrorist or mentally ill.
London, Dresden. Berlin. Hiroshima, Nagasaki.
The casualties difficult to estimate. Hiroshima:
66,000 dead, 70,000 injured. In a minute. Nagasaki:
39,000 dead, 25,000 injured. There were more people killed,
100,000, in more terrifying fashion in the firebombing
Of Tokyo. Two arms races after the ashes settled.
The other industrial countries couldn't get there
Fast enough. Contain, burn. One scramble was
For the rocket that delivers the explosion that burns humans
By the tens of thousands and poisons the earth in the process.
They were wondering if the terrorist was crazy. If he was
A terrorist, maybe he was just unhappy. The other
Challenge afterwards was how to construct machine guns
A man or a boy could carry: lightweight, compact, easy to
     assemble.
First a Russian sergeant, a Kalashnikov, clever with guns
Built one on a German model. Now the heavy machine gun.
The weapon of European imperialism through which
A few men trained in gunnery could slaughter native armies
In Africa and India and the mountains of Afghanistan,
Became "a portable weapon a child can operate."
The equalizer. So the undergunned Vietnamese insurgents
Fought off the greatest army in the world. So the Afghans
Fought off the Soviet army using Kalashnikovs the CIA
Provided to them. They were throwing powders in the fire
And dancing. Children's armies in Africa toting AK-47s
That fire thirty rounds a minute. A round is a bullet.
An estimated 500 million firearms on the earth.
100 million of them are Kalashnikov-style semi-automatics.
They were dancing in Orlando, in a club. Spring night.
Gay Pride. The relation of the total casualties to the history
Of the weapon that sent exploded metal into their bodies—
30 rounds a minute, or 40, is a beautifully made instrument,
And in America you can buy it anywhere—and into the history

Of the shaming culture that produced the idea of Gay Pride—
They were mostly young men, they were dancing in a club,
A spring night. The radio clicks on. Green fire. Blue fire.
The immense flocks of terrified birds still rising
In wave after wave above the waters in the dream time.
Crying out sharply. As the French ship breasted the vast
    interior
Of the new land. America. A radio clicks on. The Arabs,
A commentator is saying, require a heavy hand. Dancing.

D.A. Powell

DON'T TOUCH MY JUNK

I strip
for tips
it's pits
it's hit
or miss
you sit
unzip
and spit
on it
but it's
a trip
my trick?
I'll piss
I'll shit
I'll fist
yr dick
I'll lick
yr lip
till bit
by bit
yr sick
of it
I quit
at six
let's fix
let's sex
be quick
who's next
so thick
I'll rip

Rick Lupert

THE BEAVERS HAVE A CHAT

The clitoris is pure in purpose
said Mr. Beaver to Mrs. Beaver
reading off the wall of their
newly dammed dam.

I was worried about my own vagina
she responded, relieved that
he understood what she
was going through.

She took it a little too far
this moment of building between them
when she told him *my vagina is*
green water, soft pink fields,
cow mooing sun resting which is
when he interrupted her to say

Honey (beavers use that too
even though it's more known to
be spoken by bears) *I love you*
but not poetry, so much. Excuse me
while I head back up to
fetch more of these strange
February building materials
to build a little beaver nursery
for after the next time I
swim up your river.

Carolyn Cassady

POETIC PORTRAITS

7 January 1994

"I want to know
Who this 'GOD' of yours is,"
He said with a sneer
In his voice –
"Why, Allen, my dear,
It's the same one as yours.
None of us
Has any choice."

Sometime in the 60s
      (retrieved from old files)

Amazing—Allen
You teach young minds
That Art is easy—
Be a poet!
Be degenerate!
Be bitter of heart and
Shriven of soul—
Squirt words
Not from Spirit
But from spit
Doped—and acid
Semen—

Untitled III

There is a life inside of me
But I have lived another

Strains of music, sudden scenes
A certain kind of afternoon
Old flashes of an empathy
That came to pass too soon.

There is a life I meant to live
But I have lived another…

Saul White

THE FUNNY STYLE CAT

There once was a funny style cat
who used to visit me at the pad I had
up on Grant Avenue

And this funny style cat
who used to visit me at
the bottom of a forty-degree concrete walkway
with the grass growing up through the cracks
was funny

And the reason he was so funny
(which is really sad when you're a funny style cat)
is that he just sat around all the time
talking about what he was going to do

Talking up all the time to do it in

Hanging me up
like
I was a funny style cat

Michael C Ford

I NEVER HAVE A BAD DAY EXCEPT FOR THE ONES THAT END IN *Y*

I am not well thought of down the
corridors of corporate criminals.
I consider it an honor to be hated
inside the walls of an aggressive
government that calculates the
profiteering from permanent war.
I do not admire acquisitions of
conniving, conspiring uncreative
writing program spawn infested
with the mites of knowledge and
a strained bureaucracy.

I'm sick of ambitions and I wish to
remove all their wasted vestiges. I
do not own anything and do not
want to be owned by those who
own it all. I comprehend security
and indolence only because I am so
acquainted with all their repulsive
qualifications which more and
more these days begin to compete
with my own illustrative limitations.

Walking human torture chambers
are passing me by all day long on the
avenues of cultural iniquity. I stroll
into a flower shop and buy carnations
from a zombie. When I step outside I
glance up at the sky and see clouds
scudding like scullery maids carrying
slop buckets full of strychnine.

Los Angeles, California {2021}

MK Chavez

LETTER FROM ROSEMARY'S BABY

In her red room, I emerge among poppy heads
that populate the wallpaper.

Mother dreams that her bed is floating on a vast ocean.

I watch how they underdress her, this vessel
this woman undone.

I pick her because she is sacrilegious and sleeping with Satan. I
approve of her short hair and mini-skirts.
My mother is eating raw meat and upsetting the neighbors.

I am the unexpected, the leading role in hot pink.
I'm mass hysteria, the little nightmare. Men
making decisions about women's bodies.
I'm primal, baby gaze. Mother loves me
like Mary, who doesn't need Joseph.
I bring woe wherever I go.

I love a single mother
all to myself.

Gayle Brandeis

DESIRED BY ANTS

The ants want me. For the second
time this week, they swarm the panties
crumpled on the floor as I
shower. They congregate in
the crotch, hundreds of tiny bodies;
they lap up my juices
like honey. If I slipped
that underwear on, how would it feel,
literal ants in the pants?
Would they climb up inside me,
plumb the candy apple
of my cervix, would they curl
deep in my pubic hair? The thought
does not turn me on. But insects
desire me. When I go outside,
it is my arms the mosquitoes drill,
my ankles the fleas attack, every
one else unscathed. "It's because
you're so sweet," my mom used to say,
but I don't know...Sometimes I think
flies buzz around me because
they think I'm dead.

I would love to have butterflies
flap halos around my head, dragonflies
tickle at my elbows, fire flies
turn my palms to lanterns,
but it's the foul bug
that wants me, the insect
you try to step on, swat, shoo
away, the monster bug
smelling wild or rotten
sugar in my skin.

Jessica M. Wilson

PROMISCUOUS GIRL AND THE SEARCH FOR WHITE ACCEPTANCE

A girl could just give herself over in an instant;
muted magic,
hands held open for the white stem;
a promise that she belongs
and can belong
in this one moment.

Soul thrashed,
uncleansed.
A way to an origin of forgiveness for patting out the darkness
that her womb carries.

She begs at the attention,
holding each wet connection
with more purpose for her existence;
a body warming the seed
where another combination can lead to;
a better chance to belong –
fit inward
into this circumstance
of inevitable consequence.
Her body rubs against his;
nothing delicate,
or sacred in her falling tongue.

She presses skin further
away from history.
This is her moment away
from the versatile throws;
heartache in color.

She pledges to a white cock,
a usefulness
that her lips can rub away her birth;
the stamping Earth
ground on her forehead ... brooding from all that she is.
And in this instant,
something tossed out glossy with blood;
her vanquished worth,
a woe at her feet.

No closer to winning acceptance
as the door vanishes
like dried tears
or dried void
on sheets.

Ronnie Burk

1999
To Mumia Abu-Jamal

    slaveship America your mutiny held back with a radium pin. Electrocution short-circuits the amphibious arms merchant.

    up from the subterranean caverns of prehistoric water

    The History of America is written in pig's blood. Human hair entangles the story. George Washington salutes the dollar sinking into the shit holes of time. Meltdown of the chrome-plated people. Lead-encased pellets, uranium bullets, the steamy earth rumbles volcanic stones thrown into the face of Pele's fury.

    cracked visage of light

    America your torn-down houses have festered long enough! Fog takes the shapes of my ancestors massacred in the purple night flowers—henbane, belladonna, and mandrake. If nectar is nightshade I curse you with mandrake spears daubed in the earwax of Betsy Ross' vaginal membrane.

    666 emblazons a bust of Helen. Her veiled appearances on all your warships heading for conquest makes clear your Empire is destined for burnt-out Plutonic nightmare.

Kim Addonizio

CREASED MAP OF THE UNDERWORLD

Nothing is so beautiful as death,
thinks Death: stilled lark on the lawn,
its twiggy legs drawn up, squashed blossoms
of skunks and opossums on the freeway,
dog that drags itself trembling down
the front porch step, and stops
in a black-gummed grimace
before toppling into the poppies.
The ugly poppies. In Afghanistan
they are again made beautiful
by a mysterious blight. Ugly
are the arriving American soldiers, newly shorn
and checking their email,
but beautiful when face-up in the road
or their parts scattered
like bullet- or sprinkler-spray
or stellar remains. Lovely
is the nearly expired star
casting its mass into outer space,
lovelier the supernova
tearing itself apart
or collapsing like Lana Turner
in Frank O'Hara's poem.
Nothing is so beautiful as a poem
except maybe a nightingale,
thinks the poet writing about death,
sinking Lethe-wards. Lovely river
in which the names are carefully entered.
In this quadrant are the rivers of grief and fire.
Grid north. Black azimuth.
Down rivers of *Fuck you*s and orchids
steer lit hearts in little boats
gamely making their way,
spinning and flaming, flaming
and spiraling, always down—
down, the most beautiful of the directions.

La Loca

YOU SHOULD ONLY GIVE HEAD TO GUYS YOU REALLY LIKE

Hush
Pharoah in death
Bloodless
The priests' prayers are finished
The eyes of your soul meet mine
I enter your bedroom
By summon
To lead you
through the avenues of afterlife
into Heaven.

Oh God! You are so sexy
You are doing your levitation act
On linens
Caulked and malted with the
Balm and stuff
Undertakers love
And you are levitating
Nude
Lank and improper
With the threat of nirvana.

Oh Christ! You are so sexy
I stand a Sphinx
Mortared in a body of stone
Rock talons silting at the lapping spit of the Nile.
You are the East
And I cannot move my unmuscled mass
Toward a theory.
I am mind and you are man.
And your soul's eyelashes
are long
and pretty.

Oh, I love that
Killed king
Across the Nile.
My brick shrinks to flesh
I lass-like vault
from my monumental crouch
and fall into the river
a woman

And I move toward you
Thighs folding 'neath a stale slip
cutting the Nile
Bashed westerly by stabbing waters
But I inch East
on human toes
To your windlessness.

You are nuder and closer
and the faint scent of summer orange
from your airless tomb
keeps me starting eastward
In this wet midnight.

Sire
I enter your sarcophagus, dripping.
I have brought your lost life
an apple, magic, and a freshly starched shirt.
I shoo death away.
It cannot argue because it is
Nothingness
and I am
Pola Negri.

Soul! C'mere.
These incarnations were all hieroglyph.
Now, quiver, like life.
I touch you

and there is a tumult in Cairo.
Heady with grave robbing
Heady with necromancy
Heady with the mead of sweat on your scrotum
I swipe a saxophone from the atomic age
And with goddess kisses on the reed

Suck you.
Death is deaf
but not me
I'm going to suck your dick to saxophones
And get a crush on when you come.

Your breath is on Venus
Your heart is in a back alley

Your soul penetrates your body.

Cramp, cord
Roused
The bed's muslin
scratches you aware
of
Hands gloving your groin
And your cock like a deep vowel…

Hush!
You Are
So Sexy!

you are so sweetly sexy.
One simple tremble
And I fall in love with you again
Sigh or choke

And I fall in love with you again
Wallow or lean this way or that
And I fall in love with you again

And now
The taste that flirts upon my tongue
As you send your carrier pigeon to Egypt
A second, drought
Then the Nile
and then
    my flooding mind.

Your orb, scepter and crown, restored
You sit
You stand
You banish me back to the West
Where I will creak on my haunch
Until the next time
My riddles and my antiquity
murder you
and you
Summon.

Derrick Brown

THE KUROSAWA CHAMPAGNE

Tonight
your body shook,
hurling your nightmares
back to Cambodia.
Your nightgown wisped off
into Ursa Minor.

I was left here on earth feeling alone,
paranoid about the Rapture.

Tonight
I think it is safe to say we drank too much.
Must I apologize for the volume in my slobber?
Must I apologize for the best dance moves ever?
No.

Booze is my tuition to clown college.

I swung at your purse.
It was staring at me.

I asked you to sleep in the shape of a trench
so that I might know shelter.

I drew the word surrender in the mist of your breath,
waving a white sheet around your body.

In the morning, let me put on your make-up for you,
loading your gems with mascara
then I'll tell you the truth.
I watched black ropes and tears ramble down your face.

Lady war paint.
A squad of tiny men rappelled down those snaking lines
and you said,

"Thank you for releasing all those fuckers from my life."

You have a daily pill case.
There are no pills inside.
It holds the ashes of people who burned
the moment they saw you.
The cinema we built was to play the greats
but we could never afford the power
so in the dark cinema
you painted pictures of Kurosawa.

I just stared at you like Orson Welles,
getting fat off your style.

You are a movie that keeps exploding.
You are Dante's fireplace.

We were so broke,
I'd pour tap water into your mouth,
burp against your lips
so you could have champagne.

You love champagne.
Sparring in the candlelight.

Listen—
the mathematical equivalent of a woman's beauty
is directly relational to the amount or degree
other women hate her.

You, dear, are hated.

Your boots are a soundtrack to adultery.
Thank God your feet fall in the rhythm of loyalty.

If this kills me,
slice me julienne,
uncurl my veins
and fashion yourself a noose
so I can hold you
once more.

Alexis Rhone Fancher

WHEN I ASKED HIM TO TURN ME ON HE SAID:

1. *Turn yourself on.*
His voice had that flat affect lovers get
when they're done with you.

2. *You're burning through men*, my mother warned.
Like there was a limit.

Every day, a fresh opportunity
to ruin some poor man's life.

I was on fire.

3. *I'd take a bullet for you*, he told me once.
And meant it.

I didn't answer.
I tasted loneliness at last.

4. And he, behind me,
palms on my ass, riding.

5. (That night) I fell asleep with the TV remote
between my legs.

When I awoke, he was gone.

6. If he knew what I would write about him,
he'd have hated me sooner.

7. Sometimes, the person you'd take a bullet for
is the one behind the gun.

Joe Pachinko

GOD IS AN ASSHOLE

In my dream I had been sent to India.
I don't know why.
I would talk to people
and they would look at me
but they wouldn't respond no matter what I said.
A little Indian boy was very mad at me,
I don't know why,
but when I picked him up and put him
on my shoulder
he was happy and forgave me everything
whatever it was,
and he led me on a tour,
and I could see all the funeral ghats along the Ganges
and the temples and the palaces.
He led me through the market and the slums,
and the dead bodies, and the suffering
and talked to me,
he said, "What you don't understand is that there is
life on Earth and there is life with God, and God is an
asshole. Here we understand that."

"I always knew that God was an asshole," I said.

"That makes you one of us," he said.

Annette Cruz

IT SUCKED BEING A TEENAGER IN THE 80s

I was molested at 14
Pregnant at 15
Gave birth to my son at 16
Got kicked out of my home at 17
Gave birth to my daughter at 18
Moved into my first apartment at 19
And had a nervous breakdown at 20

I asked my mom for birth control in the 80's
But we were Catholic
Instead she held bible study in our dining room every Wednesday
In hopes it would help curb my very active libido
I asked my mom to help me get an abortion in the 80's
But we were Catholic
She made me keep it even though I wanted to
graduate from high school and go on to college,
ITT, I really believed computers were the future
Instead she forbade my baby's daddy from coming over and
I had to pray the rosary 3 nights a week on my knees
So God could forgive me and the shame
I brought to my family

My baby's daddy loved PCP in the 80's
And he was serving 16 months at Eastlake for stealing cars
by the time our son was 6 months old
I moved out of his Mama Chica's house when
He got released from juvenile detention
and came back home to me
with a growing belly
Carrying another boy's baby
That was due in just two little months.
He was a piece of shit anyway,
As he stole money from my wallet
That I had earned from working
At McDonald's in South Pasadena.

Selling my grandmother's ring,
Given to her by my grandfather
When they were young
and in love.
That ring was given to me
by her.

I confronted my molester in the 80's
And asked him why did he do it…
It was love, he said…
And I realized then HE was the reason
I was so promiscuous
I was not a whore or a slut
And I was especially not looking for love
I was running as far as I could
From the memory of
That grown man
Who did a lot of cocaine in the 80's,
My father…
Son of my grandmother, the ring giver,
You know, that ring…given to me by her.
She gave birth to that grown man
Who was bolder than any junior high school boy
I had ever known.
As he laid his hands and mouth up on my body.
I did get him to stop his rape
But it didn't stop me from becoming a victim.
It kept me secretly tied to my obsession
With taboo pleasures
But we were Catholic
And coming to terms with perversions
Isn't something Catholics do,
especially in the 80's.

Charles Webb

MAN CLAIMING TO BE TARZAN ARRESTED AGAIN
　　—*The Los Angeles Times*

How convict Tarzan of a crime?
Tarzan is King of the Jungle.
Kings decide what a crime is.

The *tracking app* cops used to find him
when he "stole" a woman's phone
only shows how weak they are.

Simba wouldn't need an *app* to track.
He would have crunched the phone
and snapped the woman's neck.

Tarzan showed mercy like a king.
He should have been driven
to lunch at Spago's, not to jail.

Bad people have trapped the jungle
in a zoo. The juju-powder
"John Rodenborn, 37," hoovered up

his nose, opened his eyes. Neither
Cheeta and his apes, nor Tantor
and his elephants could escape

to heed their king's yodeling cry.
That is why zookeepers found him
shirtless, mud-caked, swinging

tree to tree above the monkey
house, calling to the trapped,
chittering creatures, "Follow me."

Laurel Ann Bogen

LULLABY FOR AN IMAGINED CHILD

I never water my plants
so what makes you think
you would be any different?

It's not that I did not try —
the first attempt was
an orchid — a gift that required
a commitment —
and directions to be followed

I followed

then the amaryllis,
the hydrangea,
three types of ferns.

Caveat emptor
they say

I knew I would make
even the most
prickly cactus shrivel.

I have no manual,
O zygote,
O whim of imagination
that could sprout
offspring that thrive

Much rather spawn
poetry, croon
hush little poem
don't you cry
Mama's gonna sing
this lullaby.

Much easier to birth
to care for
to put down
and shelve.

Tony Scibella

SPRING SWING

rain wet
fresh born
the crop seeded
& brite green things shoot for the sun
lite winks on us

i am weak too
new
colt-like skinny legs
wobble bones in the air
tremble to support my own weight

chesty
heart-beat
new word world
springtime sattidy nite
fiddle-stringed knife notes
the wired fingers
box blowin

we seek to speak
to all green thumbs
who look to the sun
& feel the rain in the face
moon juice
partial to poets

the lady's tears

Mike Sonksen

VENICE BY THE SEA

Venice by the Sea was built by Abbot Kinney
        at the turn of the 20th Century.
A Utopian community modeled after its namesake in Italy.
        Canals were cut through marshes
                as part of Kinney's quest
                      to build Coney Island of the West.

Beach cottages replaced tents, gondolas were in the Canals,
        roller coasters graced the waterfront,
                gambling ships sailed in the ocean,
        escapism the ethos in Prohibition.
Venice was a separate city for a generation,   the inevitable annexation
                into Los Angeles was because of politics.

The World Wars & aerospace industry left Venice a rundown beach town
                affectionately known as the Slum by the Sea.
Poverty gave way to poetry, the affordable, empty   streets
        opened the door for   a generation of Beats.

The Holy Barbarians of Lawrence Lipton,   gathered in the Gas House &
Venice West,
                it wasn't a place for squares to rest.
Stuart Perkoff yelled poems nonstop, poetry & Live jazz was with Kenneth
Rexroth,
                they almost banned the bongos.
              The lights went dark at Pacific Ocean Park.

Jim Morrison & the Doors kept the flame alive,
        Dogtown & Z Boys skated for their life
                redefining skate cool in an empty swimming

                    pool.

Poets like John Thomas & Philomene Long, seventies singers
of the Venice
song,
        Carrying on the legacy of Venice beats, it's always been
Bohemia on the
Beach.
The flame stayed stoked at Beyond Baroque
with poets like John Harris & Michael C. Ford.
        Wednesday Night's Poetry Workshop bridged from Poetry
to Punk Rock.

The Venice Boardwalk always rocks,   Hollywood Blvd.'s
evil twin sister,
Open-air vendors, performers, fortune tellers, beach dwellers,
incense sellers
backpackers,
                        Roller bladers, tattoo artists & skaters.
Drummers in the drum circle, weight lifters, Muscle Beach: The
Mecca of
BodyBuilding,
Abbott Kinney hipsters, homeless grifters, nomads living in vans,
Transcendental
vagabonds,
                                all composers of the
Venice song.

Walking through Venice it's a coastal village before redevelopment
everybody
was chilling
        now Fortress Architecture is in the mix International
style & New
Brutalists.

The Shoreline Crips & Venice 13 have been on the scene for
a few generations,
                        Oakwood's seen
gentrification.
        Venice's original area of African-Americans
        now has wealthy landowners & McMansions.

Small World Books & the Talking Stick, bringing you back
in the dense Mozaic
Respect to Ordell Cordova & Nickie Black, Venice beats off
of Abbott Kinney.
   Walking through side-streets to backyard parties,
      barbecue after barbecue,
        Venice Beach zeitgeist is nightlife & culture
on the water.
Suicidal Tendencies to Teena Marie, a landscape for music & poetry.

Venice was lawless & still can be, poets wandering from party
to party
    yelling nonstop poetry, freestyle dancing &
  improvising
     Venice vibes rising, Venice inspires vibing,
   It's been that way for a Century, Welcome to Venice
by the
Sea.

Philomene Long

MIRRORS ARE SLEEPING WINDS

Mirrors are
Sleeping winds
In this glass room
Its window
Dreams into frost
Hours after hours pass
I sit before it
Death
Swinging in slowly
In her pleated black skirt
The night, black
As patent leather shoes
It is palatable, the sounds
Of the newly dead
Grinding their teeth
In a grin of relief
Too soon to be ghosts
Too late to speak
As I, neither fully dead
Nor fully alive
Sit with them
Upon their marble lakes
I do not feel
Their marble kisses
Upon the poems
Steaming on
My marble lips

Peter Coyote

FLAGS

Flags are everywhere.
Tied to cars, stitched to clothes, strapped
to twisted girders, fanning the air
where silver needles have pierced
the steel ribs of an idea, tossing hope
to the teeth of gravity, cinching
the collar on a world straining to breathe.
Men are lifting broken children from stones
in Beirut. A flop-eared mutt guards a human
foot in Bosnia. Stacked skulls peek
through lianas in Guatemala, while a fireman breathes
into the mouth of a dead infant in Oklahoma.
The cookies of mothers, pomegranates, musky sheets
of marriage beds, pistachios and birthday cakes
are drenched in oily smoke and iron slag. Everywhere,
electrons serve only their own will,
heavy metals float as ash. Gaps appear
in every skyline. Everywhere, flags
open their wings in the hearts
of people, flutter in the corner of my tv
while a man who thinks he is speaking,
barks, cracking the ribs of the hungry; pretending his lips
are not slick with marrow. The prep-school boys
are loose again. The palm-frond bars
are stocking up on brewskis, and gimme-hats.
Tegucicalpa, Khe San, El Mozote and Panama,
Baghdad, Kabul, Multan and Peshawar-the
syllables of their glory days clot the tongue,
stop the ears of history. The Class of '55
is lonesome for iridescence and the hum
of bottle-neck flies. Soot-stained
snapshots, an upturned chair, a hand in the dust
covered by a hankie—everywhere
people are weeping and afraid,
waving flags, cursing, plotting check and mate,

as if one smooth move might rid the world
of shadows. They are burying
Jews in Tel Aviv, lofting flag-wrapped martyrs
in Ramallah, cursing the mourners in New York.
Everywhere, there is emptiness, tattered space
where someone used to saunter
or warm their hands with hot chestnuts.
Each banner is a thousand deaths somewhere
else, each flag a sword, or swooning plane,
a caress—somewhere else. Each snapping flag taps
a riddle in code: How can the heart of a people
be opened by a killer? Closed by a leader? Numbed
to suffering as it weeps? The dead
in Chile are poems. The dead
in Nicaragua are palms and vines. The dead
in Yugoslavia are stacked in Brussels,
in Baghdad are irradiated dirt. The dead
in New York are dust, drifting onto the sills
and dashboards where the glass vaporized,
dancing in freshets of air that hiss like plaintive whispers,
startling those holding their breaths, alert
for the faintest of cries from the rubble.
And the hard man with the soft brown eyes
rests in the lavender shadows of poppies,
negotiating with the Angel of Death
the requisite number of souls
to weave a flag grand enough
for Allah.

Autumn Equinox 2001

Matt Sedillo

CITY ON THE SECOND FLOOR

There is a city on the second floor
An international destination
Whose entrance is prohibited
To all those appearing
Too poor for travel
Where commerce crosses
Bridges of wire and concrete
Just above the streetlight
Rises an economy of scale
Where buildings and offices
Connect to disconnect from the world below
Here
In the space between
Worker and destination
Conversation spins profit
And no one moves without reason
And no one speaks without purpose
Here
The word is stillborn
A commodity
And the world dies anew
Here
Working stiff spend wages
In cheap imitation
Of their exploitation
Arrogant
Delusional
Walking dead
Laughingly dreaming
Of a penthouse suite
They will never reach
While staring from terraces
Towards the street below
Towards the street below

Ron Koertge

ANNUNCIATION AT PICO AND SIXTH

My partner and I pull over this possible
DUI and run her plates. It's just routine,
but something about the way she looks
in all that hopped-up light reminds me
of what my art teacher said that time
I went to city college:

In bad paintings nothing fazes Mary.
Not the wattage, not the angel, *nada*.
But in good ones, she's like this
blonde -- half-blind, a little scared,
pretty sure she hasn't done anything
to deserve all this.

Mary TallMountain

COYOTE IN THE MISSION
(In response to the painting by Harry Fonseca, 1984)

oozing machismo
elbows akimbo
foureyes groping
he cases the scene

black leather torso
stiff new blue jeans
polychrome ultra-sneaker
moonboots cover
old chicken-claw feet

jangling nailstuds hide
skinny shivery arms
stalwart heart
beats an extra **FOOM!**

slitted eyes search out
sneering enemies
somewhere in
quivering shadows

Kennon B. Raines

COSMOPOLITAN JUNGLE

Dynamic, Thrilling, Bloody, Burnt
DESTRUCTIVENESS
Creates suspense for us
As it stalks our pulse
In the vegetated and concrete jungles
Unnerving farmers in their fields
Where the sun is shining
And the cool, strong breeze is cleansing
Sparkling life is inhaled
In luxurious fast-food-chain fashion
And fashion is flaunted frequently in the streets
Gleaming with coughed up blood & morning dew
Jungle jubilant insatiable savages
Numbed by beauty & fear of napalm
Entertaining false security
Freeze-dried faith
And shackled motivation
Sophisticated savages
Esteemed and hygiene clean
Sacrificing humanity
Violently over-feeding destructiveness
Biting the feeding hand of the land
Casual flinch...
Tune out the pain of awareness

A.D. Winans

DEAD HOURS OF DAWN

Sitting here in my small apartment
winding down the morning hours
the fog blankets the city like a police dragnet

Shaman poets sing in my ears
under an imaginary bed of stars
bring back images of young women
with dresses that clung to firm thighs
damp dark cavern wet as morning dew
peach fuzz dinner drew me in
devoured me like quicksand

Born premature at home
I survived to walk the jungles of Panama
fed off North Beach Beat Mania

Now alone and eighty-five
I sit at Martha's Café with
a cup of coffee for company
as visions of the past take root
seek refuge in my memory bank

The wind sharp as a knife
propels me toward my destiny
my boyhood gone like an old jalopy
used-up rusting in an auto junkyard

I head toward the comfort of the now
nailed to the cross of the past
in the language of the present
with no words to light the fire like
a mountain climber weighed down
with a heavy backpack

Vague recollections of my mother
holding me in her arms
the chill of a startled waking
the tongue of dawn cold as dry ice

A dog barks at an imaginary enemy
a cat yawns in boredom
the universe draws new boundary lines
fragile as a newborn baby

The monkey rides his master's back
fearful police lock and load their guns
black boys moving targets in the night

Voter suppression laws
to keep the power structure intact
southern barbecues with rednecks
hungry for black boy stew
gone the passion of revolution
sell out satisfaction to the status quo

The night hounds of death stumble
into the light of day
the rich roast the poor like a pig on a spit
the war machine moneymakers
fuel the cash registers of America
with the blood of our youth

The Roman Senate proceeds unabated
turn out gladiators like machinery parts
endless parades marching bands waving flags
played out like a Disneyland production
slaves without chains
government without representation
this nation of criminal politicians

The ghost of Custer rises like
a creature from the lagoon
creeps through the night like
a faceless Santa Claus with
a bag of Indian scalps

Allah competes with the Pope
for the rights to the head of Jesus
beheaded by ISIS barbarians
back from a night of slaughter

The congregation stumbles like
a drunk into the future
as I wait for the night hours
try to shut out the demons of insomnia

The all-night carousel runs non-stop
spits out gold rings at the patrons
the ticket-taker caught in the stampede

The holy of the unholy money makers
hide inside their gold temples
pass new laws that feed on the bones
of the poor and dispossessed

A future where animals turn into animal crackers
and wingless birds hop frantically around
the thanksgiving dinner table
knifes stuck in their breasts waiting
to be served as a holiday feast

The angels occupy the box-seats at Yankee Stadium
God sends down a bolt of lightning
dismayed at the flawed diamond
he created in his image

Linda J. Albertano

PROGRESS

I dunno. Where
did it all start?
We shoulda built a barricade
against all this inventive
intellect.
    Phonograph records?
        Teletype machines?
            Smart Phones?

Impale their metal carcasses on flame-
hardened stakes! Where
was Dracula
when we needed him?

I see Madame Curie -- lit
from within by radio-
active fireflies -- sifting
through mountains of pitchblende
for the stuff of the 10th
dimension!
    Nuclear Submarines?
        Three Mile Island?
            Neutron Bombs?

I see Gibson Girl touch
tip of paintbrush to lip to form
point perfect. Pandora
putting faces on the luminous
dials of watches. Oh, radium,
radium! When
did your kiss become
cancer?

Perhaps
Inquisitors were correct when
they quashed Galileo
and Copernicus for dangerous
thought.
        Attack Drones?
                Artificial Intelligence?
                      Pandemic Virology?

Humankind grunts, "must monkey
with gears of doom."
At least jam
scissors of science into electrical
outlets of infinity.

Karl Marx said machines would free
the enslaved. We could loll
forever in the arms of
Philosophy.

Hah!

Each new time-
saving instrument only speeds
the revolutions of our helpless labors.

Question:
If Dolphins had prehensile
thumbs
and the wheel, would
<u>they</u> have come
to this?

We're a blur
on the turn-
table of time. Spinning
into butter. Spinning
into white illumination. Is <u>that</u>
what is meant by
Nirvana? Oh,

well. Even intelligent
toddlers will soon have
the bomb.

1000 light
years away may
the sight of our disintegrating
Super Nova instruct other
advanced civilizations.

There's such a thing
as being too
damned smart for your own damned
good.
We're <u>brilliant</u> insects. I only hope
our fossils can fuel alien
spacecraft
for millennia to come!

Gary Lemons

RETURNING

A child stands in wonder
At a thing she thought lived
Only in her dreams—she sees
Secret thunder inside a glass bowl
Where soft little turtles brought
Home in plastic bags explore
Transparent prison walls.

The half-life of life is less than
The blink of the turtle's eye—old
And wise in the egg—born knowing the
Inexhaustible spirit—expecting no
Quarter from things that breathe—rocked
By the salt of its blood that is
All that's left of its home—

The turtles tremble as the toilet
Flushes them back to ancestral spirits
Beneath the sea—like leaves from a burning tree
Floating through space to set another tree
On fire—they will not be silenced.

Or Paul—on the road to Damascus—
Cursing and swatting at angels
While becoming one.

Billy Burgos

MOVIE PHYSICS

At Twelve years old we only
play hangman with the stars,
draw imaginary legs and nooses,
chalk lines from one twinkle to another.

Then we find out truths with the
help of movie physics, becoming
armchair scientists along with what
happens daily in the red soil below us.

The geometry of a gun,
The way it looks from the nozzle end,
about black holes and white faces,

how they both eat and extinguish darkness,
the science of a knee against the
crook of a neck and how long it
takes to stifle a man's life force,

space time and the way Mars
resembles a desert between
L.A. and Las Vegas.
At 48 I am aware of it all.

Dark Matter is as infinite
as all the dark faces around me.
The humanity of love is the
polar opposite of racism and hate.

It takes 2400 rpms to spin a
propeller on the surface of Mars,
Which is barely enough force to
change a mind on earth's surface.

Suzi Kaplan Olmstead

KAMALA HARRIS IN DEGREES OF KEVIN BACON

Kamala Harris just got elected Vice President of the United States

I've been waiting for a woman to get to the White House
Since I campaigned for Shirley Chisholm
And scandalized El Rodeo Elementary School's third grade
I got to talk to her on the phone once
When she was District Attorney of San Francisco
"I'm not going to prosecute you,"
She said
"Thank You"
I said
I quit using drugs after that
Went to rehab
Well, six months later
And again five months after that
After two trips to the ICU
[Went to rehab twice]
Stayed in San Diego rehab for nine months
(Saved my life)
That conversation with Kamala Harris
Was way cooler
Than the time my brother skied over Gerald Ford's ski boots
(When he was about twelve)
And got surrounded by the Secret Service
Because a Harris phone call is worth (at least) five Fords

November 7, 2020

Bill Mohr

GOOD WORK, IF YOU CAN GET IT

I work for the secret service
of imagination. The president,
who is limited to a term of three hours,
can walk around completely unafraid,
talking with people, telling jokes,
and just being happy, so it's a pretty easy job
protecting them after the vote comes in
and the announcement's tacked on a bulletin board
next to lost dog and parrot flyers, saying the woman
who just finished painting a still-life
of her baby's diapers has been elected
president of imagination from 10am
to 1pm tomorrow, so get the inaugural
music planned, swirl up the volume.
I've never come close to being elected president
of imagination. I'm too grouchy
to run a campaign, although if I could get
a little more mellow at least here's a distinction
that doesn't require a lot of money or awards
to be nominated, but I'm enlisted in its secret service
and I'm very honored to be trusted
with that responsibility. Because the office
moves so much, it's easier for the President
to come to me, than for me to go to the president,
though this complicates other eccentricities.
Say I go to a reading, or an art opening,
I'm not just enjoying myself. I'm vigilant,
every syllable, every brushstroke
has to be assessed for its nektonic potential
to make somebody happy or joyous
or do something foolish that would harm society
like spend the rest of their lives creating art
when they should only be giving three
or five hours a week to it,
but usually, I'm not on duty.

Whoever is reading or showing their paintings
is a former president, and I don't have to guard them
They're on their own. I woke up this morning,
once again, happy and rested, because, as I write this line,
President Guillaume Raidillon is in Montreal,
and there's no way I can get there in time to do the job,
so I get to keep writing this poem,
I know you don't think this is a real job,
but it is. I had to promise I'd be willing to die
for whoever has the office, whether
they're language-centered performance artists or landscape
painters; I couldn't say, I don't like that kind of work.
I have to be willing to hurl myself in front of any antagonist
in order to protect this artist and I freely took that vow,
but even under duress I'd never make the same promise
for a real president, because I've already gotten shot at too much
and I'm tired of taking the bullet for someone else's greed
I'm tired of taking the bullet of credit card usury
I'm tired of taking a big bullet in my small toe
I'm tired of taking a small bullet in my big toe
I'm tired of taking a military budget's smirking bullet
and the fossil fuel bullet of particulates in my lungs.
It's hard to breathe knowing 87 year old women
are floundering in urine soaked sheets
at this very moment, women who worked all their lives
and deserve to be massaged every morning
with sweet oils, to have the hands of kind women
rub their shoulders and stroke each finger,
but who will not be touched for the rest of their lives
because loan sharks in Congress proclaim
we only have enough money
to murder and imprison young men.
I'm tired of taking the bullet of circular grief
and remorseless knowledge.

Paul Corman-Roberts

THE EXPLANATION OF PRETTY MUCH EVERYTHING

    still I can't help but think you
contain not multitudes
    nor even all worlds
but all the galaxies
all the universes
and all the ultra-universes.

you manifest the spiral,
not a cycle but a vector
an echo
in every medium
we have ever encountered

this is not motion
    so much as
it is frequency
bits and pieces of you
cramming yourself out of and into
the perceptible there
    and there
between the Scylla of your wavelengths
and the Charybdis of your anti-matters

              there is where all the philosophers and
              shamans and
              alchemists and visionaries and poets rend
              their hearts
              and dash their minds against the impossibly
              dense
              contradiction of existence.

It can't be easy
cycling in and out
of all the dimensions
relative to your journey

>   but I want to be among the first
>   from my dank cubbyhole to thank you
>   for all of the hard work you are forever
>   birthing
>   these armadas of Prince Caspians
>   forever sailing
>   toward the gravitational barriers
>   where oceans of poppies and poesies
>   inevitably smother our brave/lonely vessels
>   in pollen and nectar
>   never to return.

Around and around we still go
little foundations of you with whom I surely share bits
    w/Christ w/Buddha w/Krishna w/Hypatia
    and the first opposed thumb primate
    to discover the practical value of murder

    it is you whom all of us share

and so once more unto your
long night's journey into day
preoccupied as you remain
eddying in the fringe cul-de-sac's
on the edge of town
on the perimeter of a campfire
where cold and dark things reflect
just enough candescent light
to keep you hypnotized,
    horrified
    and everything between

just long enough to keep the rest of us
hanging around
which goes a long way toward
understanding the explanation
of pretty much everything.

Ellaraine Lockie

THEN AND NOW

I don't tell my daughters
At 18 I knew my way
around a parked car
And the boy who parked it
That I was dressed up
Ready to go whenever he was
Soon dressed down in his front seat
The word *fuck* never spoken
in high school cliques
Or anywhere else by nice girls
A word never heard
Yet often happened

I don't tell my daughters
there was no safe sex phrase
That the only worries were whispers
from small town gossips
And shotgun weddings
that held girls hostage on wheat farms
Montana labor prisons
where their pardon was left to luck
of early withdrawal
Condemning evidence spilt
over their bellies
Allowing an escape route
out of state into a different life

I don't tell my daughters
from sheer copy-cat fear
Endorsement by demeanor
of a promiscuous generation
Where *fuck* is an extended handshake
in a sea of social gatherings
Accepted articulation
and an exercise in the ordinary

With reckless denial
of diseases and death sentences
Hell on earth that makes
Montana wheat farms into promised lands

Susan Hayden

SHE SAID, "THE HEALING METER HAS EXPIRED"

"A person is a whole person when they are good sometimes but not always, and loved by someone regardless." — Hanif Abdurraqib

She said, "His death took the life out of you."
She said, "You used to be gracious and carefree."
She said, "You've lost all of your joy. And charisma."
She said, "Everyone is waiting for the happy ending to this story."
She said, "Stop asking about my art and calling it 'my art'."
She said, "Now that you're single, your ego is out of control."
She said, "You're on some power trip with men."
She said, "You used to treat me like I was magic."
She said, "Every conversation between us was an awakening."
She said, "I didn't like it when my husband called you beautiful."
She said, "Three is an awkward number."
She said, "You used to tell me that I was beautiful."
She said, "There will be no cell phones at this dinner table."
She said, "I don't care if your teenaged son is calling you from Nepal."
She said, "You're right, I'm not a mother, so I wouldn't understand."
She said, "I care about you a great deal. But you don't make it easy."
She said, "It felt safer to be friends with you when you were married."
She said, "Our worlds used to fit together so perfectly."
She said, "I hear in grief you get a new address book.
    Well guess what? It's true."
She said, "I predict your husband's death will put you in a bad mood
    for ten years."
She said, "I'll only be sticking around for six."
She said, "I miss the Susan who wrote Thank-You notes."
She said, "I would have done anything for you."
She said, "You would have done anything for me."
She said, "I wanted to be an old lady with you in Paris,
    but I'll be going there with my other girlfriends now."

She said, "My Mom used to lock me in the closet and leave me there for hours. You kind of remind me of her."
She said, "Watching you all hunched over is a lesson in keeping my shoulders back."
She said, "Your life changed. I don't see my place in it."
She said, "Even though we go to the same therapist, she's advised me to end this friendship."
She said, "I need a break from all this sadness."
She said, "I admit, I liked you better before he died."
She said, "Sorry, but I can only show my courage in your dream."

King Daddy

FOLD

call my family
tell them I'm lost
on the sidewalk
no, it's not okay

squint to see it

on a scarred white table
in a dusty mason jar
my last easy breath
she unscrewed the lid

pulled up my shirt
fingernails painted milk white
she soft scratched my back
spelled out Wilco lyrics

until I waved a white flag
she told me to unclench
nobody wanted to be there
nobody wanted to leave

I was driving six white horses
she was spasm and honey
said burn down the house
pulled me into the fold

she

pulled me into the fold
said burn down the house
she was spasm and honey
I was driving six white horses

nobody wanted to leave
nobody wanted to be there
she told me to unclench
until I waved a white flag

spelled out Wilco lyrics
she soft scratched my back
fingernails painted milk white
pulled up my shirt

she unscrewed the lid
my last easy breath
in a dusty mason jar
on a scarred white table

squint to see it

no, it's not okay
on the sidewalk
tell them I'm lost
call my family

Brendan Constantine

UNSCHEDULED POEM

The next time you have the falling dream,
try to spread your arms like the letter Y.
Not only will you land easier, you'll keep
the picture longer; your grandparents
in their flying suits.

When someone says they've had a bad day
tell them it's because Mercury is in Petrograd.
When they correct you, say, *No, it's actually
the old name for St. Petersburg*. When they walk away,
be sure to shake your head.

This is the time we did not agree upon for poetry.
You remember, it was now.

The last time we met like this, we were strangers.
Not like today, the two of us intimate as books.
Back then, you were all about anonymity. And I
recall thinking I was in the absence of true genius.
This is much better. We should do whatever
more often.

When something vanishes – February, a voice,
the wine – believe it has a heaven because it does.
Understand what makes it hard to see is time
and time isn't distance. It's instance which means
it's always due.

The first time is unknowable, just accept it.
Here are some other things to accept: lambs, string,
bruises, the number ten, a sister, nothing, different
nothing.

Here is a riddle: There is no death if you cooperate
with death. Do not cooperate with death.

Also, right now, this is the falling dream.

Dennis Cruz

HEAD STOP

you're nervous
you should drink
got any of that
other stuff left?
you should have
a little of that..
not too much,
listen, relax
you should
have another
drink…
it's still early,
it's getting late,
that shit is all
in your head
there's no
secret message
not in that
book, or that
part of that
song
that was just
your mind
assimilating
chaos again,
don't forget
you're afraid of
chaos.
it sets you off
you're not good
with the heavy
stuff
go slow at first
don't binge
you dreamed that

and it didn't
end well,
you woke up,
remember?
waking up
is not
how you
wanted it
to end.

Yvonne de la Vega

I WRITE AND I FUCK

I write and I fuck
neither of which
make any money
yet both are
done to stay alive,
both are accessed by
keyword: LOVE
both shut down by the same

both are a gift of which neither
should be in any way abused

I fight the good fight
if it fall before me,
anything spilling
onto my path
is a full can of
clear choice. Overall I'm here to remind
that we are all in this together
see, people ask for prayer,
especially old homies gone religionistic
I never ask to what address
are your prayers sent? who
is the recipient
of my pleas
for you?
I shall never discriminate
any of the many names of
the most high I
know god is everywhere
and see, no matter what is taught
I know that yes Jesus fucking loves me
and he hears our tones, muses at human words and
doesn't care about the way it sounds as much as he can hear
the brilliance and the honesty of the tune within our hearts you

see, Jesus doesn't think in english as much as he feels our
universal music, and Jesus is fucking cool he says that
words are keys to turn on songs in muted
hearts and he can hear those prayers of
words unspoken and I'm not going
to hell for saying or
writing
fuck.

I write and I fuck, sometimes I write "fuck" and I can fucking write.
and while I never write when fucking, I truly do fuck with writing

I write and I fuck both are
divine and holy. both are a
gift each of which should
never be abused neither of
which
make any money
yet both are done
to stay alive,
both are accessed by
keyword: LOVE
both shut down by the same

Pleasant Gehman

WHITE TRASH APOCALYPSE

When the end comes honey
PLEASE
put me in a lavender Earl Schieb $99.95 paint-job Pinto
with home-made dingleball fringe around the headliner
a magnetic Mary on the padded dash a sixer of Rollin' Rock
under the passenger seat and Golden Oldies on the radio
Send me home from Carl's Jr. or beauty school
K-Mart or Zody's or the cosmetic counter at Walgreen's Drugs
in my pale blue Polyester pants-suit
with the thong bikini panty lines visible
through the flimsy fabric
and don't get too blinded by my hot pink
Dragon Lady sparkle flake
decal'd and nail charmed acrylic manicure
...yeah, they're really my own nails...
I PAID FOR 'EM, DIDN'T I?

Gimme the Home Shopping Club on the big screen TV
and mount it on the ceiling so's I can watch it
while my old man puts it to me
and afterwards, while he's in the john,
and I'm thinkin' maybe I am gonna order me
that Cubic Zirconia 24kt Gold Electroplate Tennis Bracelet
I want a plate of Ritz Crackers smeared with spray-cheese
a cold Bartles & James and a Virginia Slim...no, make that an Eve
Then I'll go and visit my ex
what a hunk, man, in his greasemonkey shirt
all rippling with muscles
his name stitched over the breast pocket, hands all black
from building a new carb for his panhead scoot
he'll slap me on the butt and call me "Bright-Eyes" - all RIGHT!

When the end comes, honey
let it be to Heart playing "Magic Man"
I'll be the one lip-synching into my hairbrush
dancing in front of my mirror
to Sheena Easton doing "Sugar Walls"
I'm gonna look out the window and see the Big One drop
and I'll be all ready for it
in my black Harley Davidson fringed halter
my stretch jeans and my feather roach-clip earrings
I got it all planned out–I'm gonna have
a cold brew in one hand
a shot of Jim Beam in the other hand
a big fat doobie in my mouth
and I'll be with...you know...my ex
proving once and for all that I really am a
Championship Mustache Rider
I'll look up all coy and stuff
flip everyone off
and meet my maker with a shit-eating grin on my face.

Jimmy Jazz

THE IMPOSSIBILITY OF AN ANTI-BANANA POEM

Writing an anti-banana poem is just bananas
This anti-banana poem got ruined by the word
banana

Big Mike! Big Mike! Where are you?

The despotic pink fist of monoculture could hit you
like it strikes the bloated tummy of uno niño de la finca
but the news (torture, poverty, malnutrition…) dissipates in the
sweet ripe fragrance

Extinction creeping across the world like a fungus can't stop
breakfast
These lines decrying the worst blue-black, rotten, stinking, filthy
banana clutched like a dildo in a deathhand
crawling with larvae you didn't see but tasted
might lead you to believe that bananas are hell
which makes them dangerous & cool &
misunderstood & full of mystery,
an adventure

Even people who don't eat bananas will tell you they are glorious
Peeled before frozen & whipped like iced cream
Bananas walk through the American dream like a bunch of giraffes
through tall grass

A white bowl of red strawberries
vividly red right through the bite
smelling like a summer rain-washed morning after clouds have
lifted &
dripping juice down the chin
onto her belly laugh in bed
as she greedily swipes one more than her share
leaving the empty white bowl
might have been a lovely anti-banana poem
until named

Bucky Sinister

SUCH A HEAVENLY WAY TO DIE

I had a mouthful of donut
coming out of Hunt's
and coming down off acid

This matte black Monte Carlo
stripped of its trim
blowing smoke out its tailpipe
like a basehead on payday
pulled up and I heard
The Queen Is Dead
the Smiths album I had to pretend to like
when I was in an art major's dorm room
trying to make out with her

The car was full of vatos
singing a Spanglish version of
"There is a Light That Never Goes Out"

I nearly lost my shit
started laughing
then they all got out
eyelids so low
they had to lean their heads back
to look at me.
I stopped laughing—
what's left of the acid
lit up my fear in light strobes

one of them started talking to me
the others went in
I couldn't understand him
not sure if he was speaking
Spanish or English
both of us fucked up
he wasn't speaking right
and I wasn't hearing right

finally it sounded clear:
I said,
why you got a picture of yourself
on your shirt

He had me there.

Tanya Ko Hong

MOTHER TONGUE

Sophistication isn't damn good to drink.
So why don't you untie my tongue
like you undress me in the dark, don't
let my ego ruin our night, don't scan betrayal
in your mind—life's not so bad
if you don't pay attention.
Reaching out in the middle of night, I don't know
what I'm trying to grasp.
When the sound of a trumpet wraps my body,
I want to speak in my mother tongue.
I don't apologize, *Sorry, sorry*
English isn't my first language...
Yes, I smell like garlic—don't kiss me,
I had kimchi— you smell, too, like scorched lamb
and limburger; let's just love each other.

Suzanne Lummis

HE REALLY

I went all gold like a lioness—I rolled over,
over, nothing could hold me but he

did. I surmised how much he wanted, I guessed—
call it intuition—how much he wanted

and where that want began. On him, nothing sank
or folded into swimming fleshiness—

his body'd made its mind up, firm. He'd caught
me from behind when my back was turned.

I went dumb as cattle. Something owned me.
My name turned to helium.

I could've been anyone, but I was something
specific, sudden, molten in this light—moon

through window glass. That was then,
before. Back then: a room, wall to wall

with another room. Next door, voices skittered,
and fattened on the air. In here, breath and muscle,

all the way along—how much he wanted me,
how often. That was then, before. For weeks,

back then, my car turned left at a certain
intersection, wheeled toward that deep L.A.

address. I no longer owned my car. It was on
some radar, his. He'd put out a sort of call: how

much he wanted, how much he had to want
me with. Meanwhile, billboards pitched the latest

Must-Have-Now. We need fuller lips. We need
lots and lots of skin. Did I say "dumb as cattle"?

Hmm? Did I say *lioness, gold, melting ore?*
Kinda, more-or-less? Or more? Did I say from night

to noon hour he ran in my blood like the violent, sucking
extract of a red flower? But that was then, before

the world snapped back and I owned it once again,
a few bits at least, a cat, TV, some gin, coupons

in a drawer. Even now, cook the moon over a low flame—
I'm there. Certain nights, when the pavement's

releasing the day's heat, I feel it beneath my fingertips
when I reach to stroke the moisture off my back—

a sort of imprint, I guess, of where he left his scent.
That was then. De-spelled

I've spilled back into the real. But before.
Before I came to my senses I came

out of my senses and, boy, he had me, he
had me, that boy, he really
            —for a while.

Neal Cassady

THIRD ANNIVERSARY POEM FROM NEAL TO CAROLYN

Spring of 1951 came, and with it the feeling of fresh beginnings and new hope. On our third wedding anniversary, Neal buttressed my optimism by writing me a silly poem, but one which showed his understanding and awareness of my feelings. He placed it beside my plate at dinner along with a piece of coloured glass. - Carolyn

---

To my April Fool's magnificent Ass
So beauteous, though overfull, as is your heart
With misery. I here make present a sliver of cut
Stained glass
Which unable to shave your behind's blubber
Might yet pierce your reservoir of hurt
Enough to make our third anniversary
A day of insight crystal clear
Combined with knowledge thru the ear
So that when this Sabbath sun descends
There'll be an understanding which portends
Henceforth a bliss that never ends
But shows up for joke the fear
That dread neurotic minds hold dear
To all the while make careful file
Of everybody's dreary food
On which they feed of selfish acts
Only to find it does no good
For conscience never has been forgot
The pacts made three years ago this day
When each to the other did say those eternal vows
That cost ten bucks
To get from you my legal—shucks. No paper.

Kitty Costello

POETIC GUIDANCE FROM DIANE DI PRIMA: A FOUND POEM*

In the morning, when you're not quite you,
ride that to other times and places
Overhear things
Trust a tiny piece of memory and keep going
Be completely on your own side

Write at the same time each day
and your body will depend on it
Nothing is as important
as writing in the time you set aside for writing

Kickstart – make a collage, sharpen pencils, light a candle
What you do with your actual cells
is more important than image
Image is more important than words
Organizing is as important as anything

Take a walk, look for clues—all senses
What happened on that very street in that very spot?
Pick a color. See it everywhere you go
Window shop for a character you might want to wear
Ask about? or to? for any poem
Think of those you're writing for,
not those who will be upset by what you write
Write the history only you know

Read read read
Read obituaries
Keep a notebook of title pages with no content
Let it come
Or pull down a book and grab a passage to start
See stuff between the lines on the page
Include present-moment interruptions in your piece
and look for coincidence
Hold the paradox

Study alchemy, biology, the society you're in
Don't understand it, don't believe it, but know it's true
Take the scary fork in the road
What is your poem's darkest secret? Its biggest fear?
Ask the I Ching, the Tarot
Write what you must never write

Bored? Hungry? Can't sit there one more minute?
You're probably on to something
Hold still through all your bad writing
through all your frightened, jealous critics
If there's something you're doing well
they'll pay you anything to stop doing it

Believe the news they never teach you
Things you hate are waiting to delight you
if you take your time to learn them
When stuck, cut in dreams, cut in comic books
Write for all beings. Write your own death poem
For heaven's sake, don't believe your opinions
Accept the limits of your body
The requirements of our life is the shape of our art.

* Gathered and arranged from notes jotted during
Diane di Prima's last poetics class series, Summer 2015

Kelly Grace Thomas

WE KNOW MONSTERS BY THEIR TEETH

> But what of a woman
> without canines. One who has lost
> the muscle of molars. Prisoner to a bite
> that only knows: *run.*

Inside this mouth I was once wolf.

> Now only a dress of pink
> shriveled gums that whisper:

Excuse me. Not here.
I'm not even here.

> The small death of letting
> go. Rest a four-letter word.
> My bed a shallow grave. Every morning
> I'm a shovel of knees, every night
> an earthworm of goodbye.
> Lifting from soil.

This is the dirt
of never coming home.

> I can remember
> when the first tooth fell.

The first time I monstered
or womaned

> and someone was there
> to watch.

Maybe I'm whatever evil you want
to name me. Maybe I'm not
the tooth.
But the empty space

                                          I tongue into small coffins
when there is no more
strength
to chew.

Diane di Prima

HE BREATHES

so I am printing out poems to send to the 26 magazines who
want them
or say they do
I figure I'd better get on it while I have the time
my book is done
at Viking even now getting messed with in unthinkable ways
and I have the time and I better use it
yesterday I went to visit a friend who's dying and that always
reminds me
get the poems out while you can, you know
and everything else for that matter
not to mention I had a dream last night that wasn't so good
so I am printing out poems and the phone rings and it's someone
from the *Examiner*
and only this morning I read the *Examiner* will soon be extinct
so I wonder
how the guy feels about that and I pick up the receiver
he says he heard Gregory Corso died last night and he wants
a quote
they always want a quote and usually I ignore them
but this time I say he had the greatest lyric gift of any of them
Allen, Jack
the greatest innate genius
yeah says the guy but you know genius and discipline don't often
go together
I have discipline the guy says but no genius
I have just finished printing a poem for Sharon Dubiago and want
to get on with it
before we all drop dead, you know? so I tell him to call Allen's office
Allen will still have an office after we're all gone
and that office will have quotes for everything I am so grateful
and he wants to know about Gregory's time in San Francisco
and I tell him to call City Lights and then I hang up
by this time my printer is spitting out old haikus
I only have 68 poems and 25 magazines want them or say they do

and I want to send at least three poems to each, so they'll have
a choice
and I'm trying to figure this out do the math when the guy
calls back
he says he got thru to Allen Ginsberg's office and the woman
who answered
said only "He Breathes!"
that's good I said and thought about Ray Bremser
and Jack Micheline not breathing and my friend in Mill Valley
and all the rest
me too, soon "She Breathes No Longer" they'll say and somebody
will mention my lyric gift but no discipline
and what a bitch I was   so I get my sweater
to go to the Asian/ American Restaurant, it's
Chinese/ Peruvian actually
but suddenly I decide I don't want to leave the house
so I cook some pasta and think about Gregory breathing in
the midwest somewhere
and while I keep writing the pasta is getting cold
and I can't help it I wish I could send him some ziti with
summer sauce
and Sara Raffetto my friend breathing not so good
Allen too
and he wasn't even Italian

8/6/34-10/25/20

Philip Lamantia

POEM FOR ANDRÉ BRETON

When we met for the last time by chance, you were with Yves Tanguy whose blue eyes were the myth for all time, in the autumn of 1944
Daylight tubes stretched to masonry on Fifth and Fifty-Seventh in the logos of onomatopoeic languages of autochthonic peoples
Never have I beheld the Everglades less dimly than today dreaming the ode to André Breton, you who surpassed all in the tasty knowables of Charles Fourier
Only the great calumet pipe for both of you We are hidden by stars and tars of this time
No one had glimpsed you great poet of my time But the look of your eyes in the horizon of northern fires turning verbal at Strawberry California
the Sierra Nevada from Mount Diablo on the rare clear day is enough of a gift to hold up over the rivers of noise
Metallic salt flies free
that "the state of grace" is never fallen
that the psychonic entities are oak leaves burnished with mysteries of marvelous love whose powers wake you with the glyph of geometric odors flaring in the siroccos about to return to Africa
Mousterian flint stones caress the airs of Timbuctu as I turn a corner of volcanic sunsets from the latest eruption of Mount Saint Helens

Will Alexander

ANTERIOR SPECULATION

Imagination equates with anterior speculation. In the higher states one need not embbrangle oneself via super-imposed reductive oscillation. Should skills persist at this level, if they become capable of bringing into view alchemical scars that seemingly hamper or renew poetic samsara, an ambling evinces itself via Indigenous understanding, a praxis magically unfolds that emanates as the zero field.

CLS Sandoval

FOR THE 'FEMINIST'

To the man living in the middle of my living room who calls
himself a feminist
If you're such a feminist, why do you always leave the toilet seat up?
If you're such a feminist, why do you eat all of our food that
you don't pay for?
If you're such a feminist, why are so many of my towels missing?
If you're such a feminist, why do you leave evidence of last
night's binge all over
   the bathroom for me to clean up?
If you're such a feminist, why do you routinely pay me your
portion of the rent
   months late? And the utilities?

To the man living in the middle of my living room who calls
himself a feminist
If you're such a feminist, why do you produce hardcore rap videos?
If you're such a feminist, why do you assume that I want to see
you naked?
If you're such a feminist, why do you sneak your girlfriend in
and out of our apartment, lying to her, saying that I'm a man
and your other girl roommate
   is a lesbian?
If you're such a feminist, why do you assume I will do your dishes?
If you're such a feminist, why do you leave excrement in the
toilet and brag
   about it on facebook?

To the man living in the middle of my living room who calls
himself a feminist
If you're such a feminist, why won't you communicate directly
with your other
   female roommate?
If you're such a feminist, why do you leave beer cans all over the
common areas?

If you're such a feminist, why won't you move your truck out of our parking
  space?
If you're such a feminist, why do you keep asking to borrow money from me?
If you're such a feminist, why do you keep trying to label ME a feminist when I
  never self-identified as a feminist?

To the man living in the middle of my living room who calls himself a feminist
If you are such a feminist, why do you keep calling yourself a feminist?

Jan Steckel

MARY'S CLUB

Velvet unpigmented skin of Portland girls.
Dog collar around a stripper's neck.
Guy at the end drinks with his apricot poodle,
its paws on the bar. Blacklights make
the dancer's white bikini glow violet.
Stage backsplash of padded leather.
Ceiling of square mirror panels.
Slot machine, video lottery
bookend the straitened space.
Juke box on stage under performers' control.
No bouncer. Sticker on the till:
"My bartender can beat up your therapist."
Back wall mural in socialist realist style:
naked longshoremen carrying huge bunches
of bananas in front of their genitals.

Three guys at the dance floor's edge
give positive critique: "You do yoga?"
"No, I only get my exercise dancing.
That's why this arm is fat,
and this one is skinny."
Splits, clicks to alt rock. No tattoos—a rarity.
Short dark bob, tortoiseshell frames,
puts glasses on tummy while spreads legs wide
creating a little bespectacled face.

"I'm a young stripper that's making my way in this world.
Any special occasion for you gentlemen?"

"Two of my best friends are here from Chicago,"
says guy at bar, hugging one of them.
"I used to be from Chicago."

Man in blazer, rocker-bottom Skechers,
sunglasses up on his head.
"Your name is Kyle?" she asks,
sweeping up the money.
"Yeah, how do you know my name?"
"You said your name."
"Oh."

A short and a tall dyke with buzz cuts roll in
with a small bearded person: shaven skull,
plaid shirt, and pointed, scuffed boots.
One of the buzz cuts wears a sweatshirt
emblazoned "Assholes live forever."
Plaid shirt sighs, "Ask about table dancing?"

Man in a rosary and fringed black leather
chats at ease with the barmaid,
who's taking her last shift for a while,
going to visit her parents in Connecticut.

Poodle lies full-length on the bar now.
White bikini gets more athletic,
hangs off the stage upside-down
in a guy's lap, thighs around his neck.
She puts his trucker hat on
as she slides down the wall to grunge.

Different-sex couple by the stage.
She's fat, white, yelling happily.
He's skinny, brown, baseball cap.
Both in athletic jerseys,
numbers on the back.
Shout goes up:
"It's Molly's birthday today!"

"Who don't like cocaine?"
asks Chicago boy, arms spread wide.
"I like cocaine," on his way out the door.

Natasha Dennerstein

PALM

It's very, very frightening in a world gone mad in a mad, mad world where youngsters have lost the cinema and the silver screen for a digital screen we'll scream and scream as the world will end in a digital apocalypse in an ending that fits like a glove in hand and top hat and tails have made way for latex microminis cinched at the waist and contoured noses and Kardashian asses plumped with implants and fat transfers from the belly to the butt in the belly of the beast and his number is 666. Six and sticks may break my bones and its an online bully world where my trauma is your trauma and I'm a precious snowflake or I will kill myself and it will be your fault and I can pretend to be dead and organize a go fund me page for the funeral expenses and run away with the funds to Sao Paulo or somewhere exotic where the living is cheap and a human life is worth about fifty dollars US and you can buy a meal for a dollar. Sex is cheap and plentiful and you can get fucked nightly by fit young things who lay their beautiful bodies down in tin roof shanties and hang their disco pants on a bamboo rod of their mother's huts when she goes off to the sweatshop to sew for designer labels and makes the eight hundred dollar blouses till she's blowsy and past it at forty-five. Spin me right round baby right round and fill my Western face with Juvaderm and other fillers, make me look forty till I'm sixty cause I move in the circles where eighty is the new sixty and his number is 666. The beast has a belly and she swims the seven seas, the leviathan, and she's mighty, crying then the salt water spurting out her blow hole is polluted with plastics and loaded with Ambien and hormones, plastic bags and detritus from the floating trash islands of the Pacific, terrific, Atlantic 'till it rises to the shore and totally swamps Pacific Island nations overnight, drowning the palaces, palm trees and shanties overnight 'till in the morning there's nothing left, mourning for a world that's only ever been there for five minutes in Milky Way time. Time has a way of fugit and blink your eyes and it's gone, a lifetime channel behind your lashes, a moisturized minute in the grand scheme of things and the Real Housewives of Planet Earth get their beauty products from palm oil from those Pacific Island nations drowned by the rising waters in the swamp time of their lives, slipping like sand through an hourglass, our glass lakes, Great Lakes,

Canada geese flying south for the winter and skating over the frozen lakes into Canada and back across the borders in green card freedom of Christian right and the home of the free till the stars and stripes see stars and stripe your bottom with a lash of self-loathing and a handful of pills in the Oxycontin Nations of the Ambien world.

Richard Loranger

3 MINUTES

I stand on a broad flat rock, 3 minutes of my life – of what? 3 minutes – a few dozen breaths, if you're counting, several dozen heartbeats. A few billion nerves firing. A small brown feather fluttering across a field. Slow drip of an old sink. My life – my what? 3 minutes waiting in a room. 3 minutes watching the tide come in on a stony beach, listening to each wave crash like a heartbeat, like a long, slow breath. 3 minutes of an engine running. 3 minutes of an exquisite cantata.

I stand on a broad flat rock, an outcropping really. 3 minutes. 3 minutes of nothing. Time an invention of the mind, if you're counting, and probably not what it seems at all. 3 minutes thinking about that. 3 minutes of bone pain, of absolute grief that lasts a year. 3 minutes of orgasm, pleasure-pulsing right out of your body, then slowly sinking back in. 3 minutes in the presence of a loved one. 3 minutes waiting in a room.

I stand on a broad flat rock, an outcropping high above a valley, late at night, well past midnight, full moon at my back and glimmers of aurora borealis flickering across the north sky, flickering just these moments, a few dozen breaths, moon behind in faint mist hemmed by a ring of rainbow this really happened, Milky Way hanging brilliantly in the West against darkest space, silent, and the stars shift imperceptibly, I mean the earth, if you're counting, and the slightest hint of dawn comes in from the East and dims the spectacle, and that's it, it's over.

Ken Wainio

WORLD NEWS BRIEF

THE SUN CAME UP SEVERAL HOURS EARLY THIS MORNING
WITNESSES REPORTED IT BEHAVING ODDLY AROUND 3 AM
IT WAS SAID TO BE LYING IN A PASTURE
ON TOP OF THE MOON
ONE WOMAN SAID THE STARS WERE ON THE GROUND
AND THE WHOLE HORIZON
LOOKED LIKE IT WAS BEING EXPLORED
WITH GIANT SEARCHLIGHTS

THREE DOGS CAUGHT FIRE ON A RANCHER'S PATIO
BUT WHEN INTERVIEWED
HE SAID THEIR BONES HAD BEEN PICKED CLEAN
BY THE LIGHT
AND HE HAD NO KNOWLEDGE
OF THEIR PRESENT WHEREABOUTS

POLICE SAY WHEN THE SUN WAS SOBER
WHEN TAKEN INTO CUSTODY THIS MORNING
AND BOOKED ON CHARGES OF DISTURBING THE PEACE
IT IS PRESENTLY BEING HELD PENDING TRIAL
BETWEEN OUR SOLAR SYSTEM
AND THE NEAREST STAR

FARMERS OFFERED TO BUY THE ROPES
HANGING FROM THE EMPTY HOLE IN THE SKY
BUT AUTHORITIES SAY THEY WILL BE
HANDED OVER TO THE CITY PLANNING COMMISSION
TO BE HOLLOWED OUT AND USED FOR SNAKEHOLES
IN THE LOCAL ZOO

THE SHADOW LEFT BY ITS ABSENCE
IS PRESENTLY BEING INVESTIGATED

Marc Olmsted

VACCINE

Inoculate hunger
Inject education
Unplug Virus X tweeting!
Mask socialism calling it
"free health care"
Drain oil abscess
from gasoline planet's arm
Social distance the cops
clubs & guns sheathed
in weeping empathy -
Police dog's head of anger
now stretched out
on massive paws

Danny Baker

DUPLICITOUS UNCONDITIONAL

deafening,
the screeching gears,
shifting intellects,
their weathervane charity
& equivocal love

crying,
as embers boil
the weathered cauldron
—love above all—
they hiss into a vacuum,
a pit slithering w/ undulating corpses
the equivalent empty
abyss
chronic night,
the stars dead

their mass,
exhausted by spite
emboldened by the scent
of selective assault
collective gang rape
delivered
w/ leering wooden smiles
beneath the altar
of inclusion, guise
of integration

fellowship
preapproved
if verified conformity
girds fragile images
reaches hearts
& numbs minds
in proper syntax
shrill print in footnotes
see below
subject to change

this bloody mob
blindly obsequious
genuflecting
to beady eyed brilliance
of illogical wiring
aiming at common targets
for absorption
for commoners, together
vilifying brothers
embraced w/ fingers crossed
& chilling smirks
refusing possession
its transgressions
hypocrisy
its original sin

their bloody prints
adorn the blade
which carves rhetoric
on the spine of the virtuous,
now limp, below
their brow
their contemptuous glare

its mirrors black,
regurgitating plagiarized aphorisms
unobstructed by binding
self-examination
reflection,
this heaving hypocrisy
thieving art
possessing it
gagging its authors
taming dada
its lapdog
snarling

these acceptors
lenient
loving
banal
objectively crass—
coopting
thieving
draining
redacting involvement
in its deadly game

detest & loathe
blanketed in a sea of love
behind a wall of buddha
squeezing
manchurian winners
thru a shrinking spigot
onto a featherbed
of half-truths
of whole lies

their little souls
their massive jealousy
rage
spite
pettiness

weakest conscripted
for realignment
they & themselves they fool
fools with books
with quotes
with the stolen art
appropriated

dissenters
near silent
their last are labored
labor camp
in labor,
the bastard children
of their inaction
final error of the victims
before their cattle car
omission

claiming champion, the horde
loudly rejecting claims of
indifference to blind justice,
watches her
her eyes closed,
her clothing shredded at her feet,
tears trickling her pallid cheeks
as once proud
& valiant & majestic wolves
slowly fail in leg snares

they the chosen,
are nothing
are nothing
but thieving pigs,
here to help you
here to help you think
here to guide your thought
here to control your movement
control your tongue
castigate your dissension,
outlaw your rebellion
w/ the brightest of smiles

their violins play chopin
vivaldi, perhaps
but their hearts
their hearts tick wagner
in its bastardized war cries
the sound of gas
fills the theater of love,
cleansed

12/25/19

Cassandra Dallett

JAILS HAVE ATM MACHINES NOW

Plastic cards buy commissary and child support.
For an extra three dollars
you can add a personal message
Don't worry about us we'll be fine
or *We love and miss you*
Happy Birthday
After we slide our credit cards
a woman behind us struggles
to shove in her few wrinkly dollar bills.

On the block the kids stay out all night
lining the stairs with hundreds of flaming prayer candles,
spray the walls for *Poodie from two six*,
Implore him in death to shine on.
Each night they bring
the biggest red heart balloons
the kind sold for valentines and high school graduations.
They fill the street with beating heart cars
double parked and spilling liquor in his memory.

When the phone rings you press five as fast as you can.
So as not to lose a precious moment of his voice.
You accept that he can only speak to you
on a police recording.
There are options, more money for more minutes.
You can buy them so he can't call anyone but you.
You pay for time with no idea what words will fill it.
How many ways can you say love or absent.
You describe reaching for his side of the bed
using his chapstick because it's the last thing
to touch the softness of his lips.
Lips, you fell on and into in a bar,
lips you woke to, like a life raft at sea.
Behind security glass cracked and dry,
they are an un-kissed desert.

You roll his chapstick on the thirst of your lips
until you reach the empty plastic.
You run your hands between your thighs
where he buried his face at night,
feel nothing but exhaustion.

Down the street the kids are rapping,
dressed up, passing blunts
blowing smoke at the unfair sky.
You place candles in your windows, burn sage
you mourn with them.
You have suffered a kind of death also.

In the morning, you pour two cups of coffee
empty his into the garden out back.
The dogs are bored with your sadness
refuse belly rubs even when offered
you look the dog in her eye
share the disappointment of you own hand
because indeed, it is not his.

You internet search the things you can and can't send him
these companies have made phone apps to send your money to jails.
These enterprises who make the packages you send your beloved,
the same who offer to send your college student modified food
products
You tell them all the ways to recreate crackers, ramen, and chips.
to pretend it is sustenance when in fact it is currency.
The first time you saw your son's college dorm it struck you
the same companies build prison cells,
prisoners build the beds and desks in both,
to house your child, your man, perhaps yourself, one day.

Outside at the memorial they are barbequing tonight.
you put chicken in the oven
can't light charcoal without your grill man.
you tell yourself you must live,
you tell yourself to write,
wait his call, wait and wait, lose weight,
memorize the number that has replaced his name,
find his white dress shirt bought for the courtroom
limp in the dryer,
walk his letters to the mailbox,
tell yourself you are living
a brain connected to a body,
a hand to put money in the machine.
A heart commodified
a special message
Don't worry about us we'll be fine

A.K. Toney

SANKOFA SCARS

No matter how funky new we get…
No matter how cool they think we are…
Am Jazz always swinging the blues in rhythm with soul.

No matter is the blackness that we cannot escape.
Time continuum ain't no present state
When we don't know what was stolen from our backpack
Picks us up and takes us to Africa's bell of six eight.
Sankofa word bird of weight, wings of her way
She fetches us up in her beak, and flies you back
To the beginning of beyond…

She got a way of pecking at our neck like naps
She got a way of making you turn our neck
And slap us on back of the head
She got a way of making us remember them whips
She got a way to make us rhyme with that rhythm
She got a way to loosen up and make us sweat that tight
She got a way with skin, wood, and metal sounding all kettles
Festivities before feast because we are festival

Even got us paying homage
Like gambling dice on our life
Vs. Divining throwing cowries for what's right
Like spilling out a little liquor for the homie
Vs. Pouring libations of pure water to our Ancestors for clarity
As in blowing them blunts to commune with our peace
Vs. Appeasing that strong cigar smoking breath giving ebo
Ashe for Spirit's ease

Sankofa ain't no Clandestine
The power of the past is a lasting knowledge
And if we don't know our story...
Future is just an unknown edge
How far is our lineage and when will it start?
Before it's too late to realize we were apart...

2021

Clint Margrave

A SUPERMARKET IN CALIFORNIA

after Allen Ginsberg

What thoughts I have of you tonight, Allen Ginsberg, as I wait outside this Trader Joe's, red lines painted across the parking lot at six-feet intervals directing me where to stand.
    In my anxious fatigue, and shopping for wishes, I head in through the sliding glass doors, dreaming of vaccination!
    What pestilence and what conundrums! Whole families shopping in fright! Aisles full of masked husbands. Wives squeezing the avocados, clueless babies in the tomatoes!—and you, Garcia Lorca, what were you doing down by the toilet paper?

    I saw you, Allen Ginsberg, gloveless, lonely old scrubber, yearning to poke among the meats in the refrigerator and eyeing the grocery boys' hygiene.
    I heard you asking questions of each: Who delivered the pork chops? What price bandannas? Are you my Angel of Death?
    I wandered in and out of the barren shelves following you, and followed in my imagination by invisible microscopic droplets.
    We strode down the empty aisles together with our disinfected carts, in solitary distance, hoarding every frozen delicacy and trying not to pass each other.

    Where are we going, Allen Ginsberg? The doors close an hour early.
What does your temperature read tonight?
    (I touch my face and dream of contagion in the supermarket and feel afraid).
    Will we walk all night through quarantined streets? The shuttered bars add shade to shade, lights on in the houses, we're all so lonely.
    Will we stroll dreaming of the lost America of last week past useless blue automobiles in driveways, home to our self-isolating cage?

Ah, dear father, immunosuppressed, lonely old courage-teacher, what America will we have after millions of lost jobs, and we go out into a smoldering world and stand watching hope disappear like oxygen from the pneumonic lungs of God?

mike m mollett

DYSTOPIAN REVENGE FOR THE NEW YEAR HELL OF IT

i will not sit in chairs any longer.
not eat tomatoes or avocados.

i will rub out my interest in sex,
music, cats, gardens, & sticks.
lie to my wife, mother, & friends.

i will sew my smiles down & shut,
give up breathing & the use of water or wine.
chop off any remaining fingers & toes,
leap off bridges gagged & in handcuffs...

shit on the table.

i will accept the role of prisoner
since there is no escaping.
no hope. no love.
NO FUN GODAMMIT.
    & you know what-- fuck it.

Julie Rogers

TENDENCIES
for Theo & Susie Saunders

Life drives me crazy. I swear
this is not my car. I don't remember
buying it, I can't afford to rent it,
I don't recall parking here.
There's never enough insurance.
I wouldn't shop here if someone
had warned me. Who knew?
Right here this gets real
existential-like, I don't
understand the stricken
world, so sad & beautiful.
All I know is somehow
I stopped here & choose to stay
to continue the tradition.
I tell myself, "Remember to stand up."
Then I look to see if I'm here
with the key... then it all
comes back. Turns out I do drive.
I even have a license.
I drive good.

9-14-21
Oakland

Terry Wolverton

TRANSIENT

I've been driving for hours past nothing.
I wonder if I've died and just don't know.
Not even birds disrupt the white sky;
no radio signals for miles.

I wonder if I've died and just don't know,
my fingers stiffened on the steering wheel.
No radio signal for miles;
to what music do the dead listen?

Fingers stiffened on the steering wheel,
I keep veering over the double yellow line.
To what music do the dead listen?
I have only old songs to sing.

I keep veering over the double yellow line;
at what point will I fall off the edge?
I have only old songs to sing,
songs of Jesus, songs of Indian maids.

At what point did I fall off the edge?
Faster I go, more the horizon recedes.
Songs of Jesus, songs of Indian maids
embedded in the whine of the tires.

Faster I go, more the horizon recedes.
Odometer rolls to a line of zeroes.
Embedded in the whine of the tires,
the lonesome echo of the world.

Odometer rolls to a line of zeroes;
not even birds disrupt the white sky.
Lonesome echoes through the world.
I've been driving for hours past nothing.

Kenneth Rexroth

FOX

The fox is very clever.
In England people dress up
Like a movie star's servants
And chase the fox on horses.
Rather, they let dogs chase him,
And they come along behind.
When the dogs have torn the fox
To pieces they rub his blood
On the faces of young girls.
If you are clever, do not
Let anybody know it,
But especially English men.

Nicelle Davis

IF SOMEONE PAINTS A PLANT, ARE THEY OBJECTIFYING IT?

Most bang-for-your-buck, clocks in between 60 to 125 dollars. These prices reside in Central America, Columbia, and Romania. I've been giving my time to a married Romanian. He's separated, but from what? His X-ish text him good morning/goodnight, so long as her bills get paid. I'm rarely paid, even for socialist work. He sends me articles with titles such as "Is Love Just a Psychological Trick?" that concludes with "Romantic love is a lie we can't avoid." I've been shopping for plants based on women's rates. Goal: to have a plant for each pussy price-point before money breaks and the poor bleed for it. I text Romania, *Viagra you dick*, but send *live love* instead. What can I say, I like him. Is there an article for that?

When you eat a pepper, do you think about how it was once a living plant?

I was contemplating telling you about the box of body parts I've collected off my son—how much of it I've tried (post labor licked, piece of umbilical cord chewed, the wish of an eyelash swallowed). I do like the sweat and ache of pepper—the hurt of seeds. I'd like to know what's in your stomach, now that I've disclosed who's missing from mine. Such exchanges result in friendship—a truth and dare stock market. When my son was born, I made a wall of Jordans. That is, I pasted endless found pictures of starving kids from North Korea on my bedroom wall. I named them all Jordan, like the river. My husband stopped coming to bed, and instead spent all nights with porn. When I eat, I think of emptiness. You?

Which soil improves your sex life?

Soil is the number 1 killer of house plants. Sure, it holds roots, feeds leaves, but suffocates them too. This is what the descendants of gravity do: drown on dry land. Best sex I ever had, never made me orgasm. Life is bad math, I show my work, but the equations never solve. I'm not one to crash a party. He called to say, *I miss you.*

I care about you. Can we talk? But sounded mad about it. I watched the Met Gala wear several sweatshops in one night. I'm about to send invitations for a gardening party. Everyone is required to dress in Goodwill Prom attire and plant a tree. That's how much I love/hate the dirt under my nails. I'll put these nails on you—there's something like sex in that—so come on. Come on.

Do you want to be cut off from your leaf family?

You should write a short story about that, and by that my friend means: there is nothing a little boy won't do to get his biological father back. If there is a gun in the room—a boy becomes the shot—no need for a trigger. Living is a sort of bullet. My brother is the stepfather in the barrel. If I were to guess—he will keep the gun but put a ring on it. I drove out to compare social service notes. Between born and adult narratives, I thought I'd be a social worker. Isn't it humiliating when they open your fridge? Know this: it's important to always have fresh broccoli in the fridge, targeted or not. *Just don't make it about you,* my friend says, *it ruins everything.*

If you were soil, would you want to be inside? Are houses sexy?

Silphium is the origin of our ubiquitous heart symbol. Harvested to extinction, Romans valued the plant so they used it on their coinage. An early form of contraception, it doubled as aphrodisiac. Count all the values found in blooms and roots. At 42 I'm making a 2 AM tour of CVS. It's a world of plan B under fluorescent lights. We all lurch between candy bars and Fireball bottles. No one makes eye contact. I can describe the floor. Gray flecked tiles with sneaker streaks. The 15th tile on aisle 8 is cracked in the upper left corner. The greeting cards are stacked like a Colosseum of embossed hearts. Tonight, three bodies are heaped at the front door under blankets, even in 100 plus degrees. We all crave privacy, but tonight I'll settle for red vines.

* "plant questions" provided by poet Hanna Pachman

Gerald Locklin

THE ICEBERG THEORY

all the food critics hate iceberg lettuce.
you'd think romaine was descended from
opheus's laurel wreath,
you'd think raw spinach had all the nutritional
benefits attributed to it by popeye,
not to mention aesthetic subtleties worthy of
verlaine and debussy.
they'll even salivate over chopped red cabbage
just to disparage poor old mr. iceberg lettuce.

I guess the problem is
it's just too common for them.
it doesn't matter that it tastes good,
has a satisfying crunchy texture,
holds its freshness,
and has crevices for the dressing,
whereas the darker, leafier varieties
are often bitter, gritty, and flat.
it just isn't different *enough*, and
it's too goddamn *american*.

of course a critic has to criticize:
a critic has to have something to say.
perhaps that's why literary critics
purport to find interesting
so much contemporary poetry
that just bores the shit out of me.

at any rate, I really enjoy a salad
with plenty of chunky iceberg lettuce,
the more the merrier,
drenched in an italian or roquefort dressing.
and the poems I enjoy are those I don't have
to pretend that I'm enjoying.

Aram Saroyan

LIFE IS A DREAM

Life is a dream.
Boulders on the beach assume the form
Of animals. No man is certain. Death
Speaks in the wings, coaching, prompting
Emotion, the love of wood
Burning, the child's face waiting, laughing.
The sun comes up so many times, lighting
The life that is there to be seen.
We have been traveling through this tunnel
In eternity. Rocks persistently speak
To us, saying something so pure it is only
Feeling. This and that, this and that.
The buildings of the mind shut down
Before the advance of this truth.
We are here for good. There is no one
To be us instead. We are alive and dead.

S.A. Griffin

GLORY TO THE HEROES
for the people of Ukraine
for Bert de Vries

armed with an inspired lunacy
Putin is his own god
a nightmare for the modern era

as his terror campaign moves forward
the cult of war grows inside sovereign borders
where all thoughts have been tried
and found guilty

the carriers of plague with looks that kill
have landed with their tortured reward
lost lives on parade collapse in despair
as the people greet their makers of fear

ritualized by the underwriters of conflict
the authorities of speech broadcast
the intercepted letters of family and friends

history bends before the orthodoxy of bombs
flowers of evil executing a catechism of calculated risk
blossom with a bright and terrible lust
a global light of muted lifetimes
baked into the sacred tapestry of night

all the quiet stars falling like iron dice
tumbling into trap doors
of agony and tears
ever
after

March 1, 2022

Bob Flanagan

THE WEDDING OF EVERYTHING

Today looks much like
the rest: simple,
a handy kind of day,
a meat and potatoes day.
The bright buildings of the past
are launched upward
into an unrumpled sky, ordinary
beyond our wildest dreams.
Personality takes off
into the blue. No mail
today: things: everything
groping towards us
like 3-D. Oranges
as orange as crayons.
A moldy piece of bread.
Junk. And the birds
will sing sing sing.
I can almost understand
a day like this.
My troubles seem so puny.
Delicious day, I will eat you up
like a mountain of white cake,
chunk by chunk.
I've got new shoe laces.
My feet slip into my shoes
over and over again.
So easy. Everything
pleasing me, sliding down
my throat (those soft
boiled eggs) the way I slide
into this day. CRACK!
That's what I mean.
CRACK! the way a baseball
smacks a bat. and THUMP,
the way it snuggles into a mitt.

A day is as a day does,
and this day, like the rest,
is leaving, and everything
grows sleepy.
The sun rises to a place
in the sky, and leaves;
and behind it leaves
a blind spot:
the purple sun, blooming,
cut down and tossed like a bouquet.
Congratulations, everything

Joanne Kyger

DESTRUCTION

First of all do you remember the way a bear goes through
a cabin when nobody is home? He goes through
the front door. I mean he really goes *through* it. Then
he takes the cupboard off the wall and eats a can of lard.

He eats all the apples, limes, dates, bottled decaffeinated
coffee, and 35 pounds of granola. The asparagus soup cans
fall to the floor. Yum! He chomps up Norwegian crackers
stashed for the winter. And the bouillon, salt, pepper,
paprika, garlic, onions, potatoes.

                        He rips the Green Tara
poster from the wall. Tries the Coleman Mustard. Spills
the ink, tracks in the flour. Goes up stairs and takes
a shit. Rips open the water bed, eats the incense and
drinks the perfume. Knocks over the Japanese tansu
and the Persian miniature of a man on horseback watching
a woman bathing.

       Knocks Shelter, Whole Earth Catalogue,
Planet Drum, Northern Mists, Truck Tracks, and
Women's Sports into the oozing water bed mess.

                               He goes
down stairs and out the back wall. He keeps on going
for a long way and finds a good cave to sleep it all off.
Luckily he ate the whole medicine cabinet, including the stash
of LSD, Peyote, Psilocybin, Amanita, Benzedrine, Valium
and aspirin.

Dorianne Laux

ANOTHER EXERCISE IN LOVE

—after Diane di Prima

I can't remember his name, or my own,
but his hair built an alter to dreams
while he slept, bleary-eyed
in the breeze from the window, dawn
coloring his face. Oh the pleasure
he brought me the gift of his body,
dark as eggplant with that glossy
sheen, his cries like a distant city
on fire, or the ocean in moonlight
making its watery path. Now's he's
no more than a scarf unfurling
in wind, a feeling I get when
I see certain horses galloping
through a field of bronze grass,
snorting globes of winter breath,
his chest rippling as he runs.

Eric Brown

THE TRANSFORMING WAYS

I wish I could turn into a doodlebug, the guy with the protective armor casing who rolls up into a ball when you touch him; he's so small his poops are the size of a pinhead--wow!

I wish I could turn into an ant, so I could ask the other ants, how did you figure out that you could wait on that leaf on the vine on my front gate, until the wind moved that branch on that tree until it touched the leaf, and you could hop on? Where's your walkie-talkies?

I wish I could turn into a clown fish, because then my body would be covered in a protective mucus and anemone couldn't sting me, then I'd change into a marine biologist, and rename the clown fish, because he doesn't really look like a clown.

Then, a hummingbird, not to show off my eighty wingbeats per second, or twelve hundred heartbeats per minute, both of which are very showoffable things, but for the cool colors and cool names, like shining sunbeam, and glittering bellied emerald;

a whale, so I would have a tongue bigger than an elephant; can you imagine, having a tongue that was bigger than an elephant? It's exhausting just to imagine it.

If I ever learn to master the transforming ways, I'd turn into pongo pygmaeus, the orangutan, whose arms are so very long, who travels throughout the jungle hardly ever touching the ground, who demonstrates infinite grace when uncurling the four flaps of a banana.

I wish I could turn into a cat so I could purr, then get onto someone crying, to test the theory that you can't cry with a purring cat in your lap;

then I would turn into a pregnant female a, b, c or d and donate some babies to these endangered species, which are "in danger" of becoming extinct, which is a fancy word for dead.

And before it was time to change back into myself, I'd become a zookeeper, just long enough to unlock all the cages and let everyone go free!

Pam Ward

STELLA ON FRIDAY

She was walking fast fast fast
boom shaka booty doing 50
down the concrete
stepping quick
in a halter
and tangerine skirt
she was hurting them clothes
hem licking viciously
over each curve
brakes slammed
and pinstriped
old men had to choke
the bus driver sat
and made everyone late
couldn't take his eyes off
that magnificent
boom snap
boom snap
busting out at the seams
stereos tuned to
that 1000 watt strut
See, when Stella walked by
when Stella's heels
slapped the street
down the block
down to Nix
trying to get her month
to month cashed
walking fast fast fast
big size twelve's shoved
in some peekaboo shoes.
See, when Stella walked through
men thought of holiday food
ham hocks, huge plates
of glistening yams

rice sleeping under some
rich smothered chops
plenty of piping hot rolls.
See, when Stella strolled by
it was Fourth of July
she had fire-crack thighs
and some cherry bombs too
and that booty
that Rhumba butt
directing traffic
feet two strong drill bits
just busting up street
hips waxing over
them cross walkin' lines
she walked fast
she walked strong
had a serious purpose
and her eyes never strayed
from the Check Cashing sign
when Stella stepped up from the curb.

Briana Muñoz

FAMOUS POETS IN THE SACK

I imagine group sex with Whitman and Poe.
Yes,
double poet penetration.

Being soft with Woolf,
tucking the hair behind her ear,
an easy grace
my lips
against her neck.

I imagine T.S. Eliot is real vanilla.
Faking an "O" with Hemingway.
That's usually how it goes with those
Hills like White Elephants toxic masculinity types.

Right?

BDSM with Plath.
Real passionate baby-making with Neruda.
(Cries when he climaxes.)
Some trippy,
lava lamp lit, LSD
bedroom times with Ginsberg.

James Joyce spitting in my mouth.
I imagine
going down on Dickinson
and get aroused.

Peggy Dobreer

A KARA: U KARA: M KARA: ITI

You don't have to know anything to begin to do nothing.

Silence is its own master. Carries its own surplus, no tonnage,

no storage, or drayage involved. Like riding the imagination

on a carpet of corrupted intervals, a difference in pitch to a chord.

The music of the spheres is mouse quiet to naught. Beat held

to crescendo realized. Passionate soprano to Gregorian chant

at vespers or louder than a sun flare through space hits earth.

When there is nowhere to escape, don't just get going.

Just be still.

Kimi Sugioka

TEMPORAL BEATITUDES

Howling is the one true song
    that eludes the fear of night and dogs
Wailing is the one true utterance
  of a divine sun
    that grapples with drips and drabs of futility
Umbrage skywalks between the branches of things that fall
    things that grow,
        things that repeat and remember
Ever so lightly, ever so tightly,
    the reins are pulled and dropped

Sudden freedom,
  sudden fear of freedom,
    sudden sight, sudden retreat
A blessing and a privilege
  the white light of summer sings arias to fall
We become moments,
  we become prayers,
    we become radiant and vital as thieves
  on the threshold of forgiveness,
a traitor and a saint living in the same shell
  blessing and cursing
    tyranny and innocence

Oh that the lake could drown these festering thoughts
  that the bindings fray and break
    and all words stretch into birdsong
We could go where the sand becomes soil and remember planting
  Remember the taste of corn melting between teeth and tongue
    The taste of safety and home
where a mountain lullabies itself to sleep
  and marries the willow and the hemlock
so all that is feral and fetal and indigent
  might finally billow in sweet relief

We may come and go
    with and without purpose
but the whole is a fragmented universe
    we carry like a dime in our pockets

Q.R. Hand Jr.

DEFENSE OFFENSE BACK FENCE

defense offense back fence and the one around the gold yard
barkin' like a devil dog keeps some on the plantation of things that

don't care for you no matter how good the bass is and stealin' home's
more den gospel no matter where you are this sound happens don't

make no matter other sounds loud as can be dis rhythmic riff is
happening and you could still hear it when armies off others

to establish deaf zones where it was loudest and people(s)
were observed dancing which when out lawed even public fidgets

6 months and humming or whistling in public 2 years of hard labor
and drummers had their hands broken as did piano players and

music news from out side was for bidden it was rumored many were
dis appeared and cleff and staff marks left on side walks or

sand dunes hinted that some thing was wrong but futures like this were
officially denied and who knows weren't there divine signs every night

and horses too like a stampede of dust and no sounds if it wasn't here
you'd think it was weird swingin' a way or taking every thing you can you

wanna get a good con duct in wars against the homies and roll
your owns in those alleys the lucky make time in make love in and no

bodies can hide from the truth being on public tv provided by cops who
never need to leave their station house and send holograms to courts and

make testimonies with those hip hop stances authorities had legally co-
opted to further blur lines and furrow brows unless you were really in

the know about what few knew and were more hungry and stodgid (sic)
what went on be for(e) only more dogged surprise could get in the way(s)

of these cogs and their mobiles as impossible as this thing you say you
want free dom justice and equality in this process you're so fast you

can't participate except in vague dusky hotels in obscure obsolete cities
where the help seemed to say none here jack and negitiators had just

started with out you again easily since they lived there and you had
trouble getting in the door till the boss sent a picture of you and

a quick finger prick check your dna be in the right places as one of
your teams is winning and other losing every bag out of tricks the trick

of bags got you and there's alotta alligators who can't see in the dark
and bump in to you if you don't pay attention to rules from a bag dad

trickle trickle about the jewels in that ring of fire gold running down
your leg in the book where it was some body's gold getting beau coup

attention in the fillipines where this was goin'' on at planting an other
preposition at the end of a sentence tho' you can be tricked 'cause

it didn't stop there a relic aspiced in deep acting thirsting still
nothing but all brazen bad not adrift but no go here don't care

for soul no matter how good the bass is and stealin' homes' more
den gospel no matter where you are this sound happen's

Henry Mortensen

INSTRUMENTS OF DECONSTRUCTION

Violins aren't used much
in Jazz
anymore.
People don't say fiddle
much
these days.
Every violin sings its own
screeching Blues.
Sheep intestines stretched to their
limit, then strung up.
Horse hair held taught by bone
meets the gut-strings.
At the right angle, the scream
is beautiful.
Piano keys resonate with
a colonial legacy:
the blood of humans and elephants;
the black wood synonymous
with a continent,
taken to Brazilian plantations
that the jungle burns for.
Hard cinder-colored blocks
and their toothy neighbors,
totems lined up in a row,
ready to pound hammers
on the backs of string legions.
In Jazz the guitar is
in the rhythm section.
Flapping picks
still resemble
their turtle-shell heritage.
Whalers ate soup and
found another source of
organic income
when blubber isn't enough.

The alloyed metals
in the horns echo
untold histories of
cave-ins and polluted rivers
behind the melody.
The drums pick up.
Stretched, cured hides
of ungulates
imitate the heartbeats
they once contained.
They move the player's sweat
now
when the band is in its groove.
The piano may be pristine
or soaked in alcohols, blood,
and nodded-off junky drool.
But there's no avoiding the sweat.
Most pieces in the strings
have blood from
mis-flicked fingers
Those strings are ready
for action.
They are thin and ready
to test their tension.
Will finger-skin
or gut-string
break first?
All the horns are full
of spit.
And the woodwinds won't
even let you play them
without an offering
of saliva drawn out
into reeds like microscope
slides.
Smokey rooms solidify
into an extra varnish—
aspirated, expelled patina,
breath and blood,
the lives and the hopes
—buried, realized, forgotten—
of the players.

The pain
needed to make
sweet screams
called music,
the pain of
this world's life
supports
the howls
spawned
from human pain.
The source and the victim,
the powerlessness
when leaving the forest
constructed lives that need
meaning
and names of new kinds
of unhappiness.
Our own yelps turned
to joy.
Bone flutes the first
evidence of new
musical sound drawn
from violence,
the pain of their species
to add to our own.
Once the instrument is out of
the maker's house,
its life is a compliment
to the lives who touch it.
You can drink
whisky and scream until
your throat bleeds,
but nothing beats a used
Stradivarius.

Nikki Blak

BLACK LIVES

When God invented sound
We are what he intended
Us with our percussion footsteps
With our gleaming trumpets
With these lungs
With these mouths
My body, a clef
His nautilus ears
A many chambered masterpiece
And all the World
Altered, added, suspended

We were born knowing how
To prism these chords
Marry triad to rustling wind
Weave between these trees, standing
Tambourine the leaves, changing
To know the difference
To modify the time
To open the corridors
Of our throats
Forever and ever
And never have to sleep
Or wonder

We are unrelenting
8 count enough to fill a glass
Thunder enough to break it's back
Hands enough to carry it
Mend
Construct
Destroy again

We, symphony of hearts
Bleed riffs
Like the ancients
And our mothers' mothers
Their eyes, notation
Captured in our collective memory
Like rainwater
Like morning
Like the tingle of sunlight
Coloring us green

Growing us big
Tuning our guitar string veins
Vibrating our bones
Puzzling us into gifts shaped like children

Jane Hirshfield

COUNTING, ON NEW YEAR'S MORNING, WHAT POWERS YET REMAIN TO ME

The world asks, as it asks daily:
And what can you make, can you do, to change my deep-broken, fractured?

I count, this first day of another year, what remains.
I have a mountain, a kitchen, two hands.

Can admire with two eyes the mountain,
actual, recalcitrant, shifting its pebbles, sheltering foxes and beetles.

Can make black-eyed peas and collards.
Can make, from last year's late-ripening persimmons, a pudding.

Can climb a stepladder, change the bulb in a track light.

For four years, I woke each day first to the mountain,
then to the question.

The feet of the new sufferings followed the feet of the old,
and still they surprised.

I brought salt, brought oil, to the question. Brought sweet tea,
brought postcards and stamps. For four years, each day, something.

Stone did not become apple. War did not become peace.
Yet joy still stays joy. Sequins stay sequins. Words still bespangle,
bewilder.

Today, I woke without answer.

The day answers, unpockets a thought from a friend—

don't despair of this falling world, not yet   didn't it give you the asking

G. Murray Thomas

DEATH TO THE REAL WORLD

Death to cars.
Death to needing a car
    to get to the car dealer
    to buy a car.
Death to "you need a car."
Death to everyone who tells you
    you need a car.
To everyone who wouldn't think of going
    anywhere without a car.
Death to everyone who drives two blocks
    to the store
    to the beach
    to the health club.
Death to smog, freeways, accidents,
    traffic jams
    traffic reports
    traffic lights
    traffic school
    traffic cops.
Death to car dealers.
Death to trade-ins
    used cars
    new cars
    factory rebates
    nothing down
    $50 a month
    on approved financing
    on approved financing
    on approved financing—
Death to approved financing.

Death to credit.
Death to "you need credit
   to get credit."
Death to credit reports
   credit cards
   credit ratings
   credibility.
Death to everyone who wants credit
   so they can have more than they can afford.
Death to everyone who has credit
   so they don't have to ask what they can afford.
Death to everyone who wants things
   they won't work for.
Death to everyone who wants things.

Death to jobs.
Death to "you need a job to get experience,
   you need experience to get a job."
Death to 8 hr. days, 10 hr. days, 12 hr. days,
   to 30 hr. workweeks
   40 hr. workweeks
   60 hr. workweeks.
Death to overtime
   when you want a vacation,
and layoffs
   when you're already broke.
Death to plant closings,
   restaurant openings,
   time cards
   time clocks
   time to get up
   time to go to work
   part time
   full time
   overtime
   double time
   Miller time
   out of time.
Out of mind
   out of money.

Death to money.
Death to "you need money
    to make money."
Death to the rich get rich,
    while the poor get poorer,
    have children,
    are miserable.
Death to everyone who is not poor
    yet is miserable
    because they are not rich.
Death to everyone who is rich
    and miserable anyway.
Death to everyone who thinks their miser
    is caused by money.

Death to cars, credit, jobs, money.
Death to the real world.

Lee Rossi

CALIFORNIA ORANGE LIGHT SUTRA

> *"The need gotta be / so deep"*
> —Yusef Komunyakaa

If you love it
it will soon be gone
aphids on roses
rust on the corn
so love it deep
or let it go
before it sinks
its roots
deep in the splayed
arteries and veins
and drives the tongue root
vibrating into silken air
If you love it
love it deep
into the darkness
where water gathers
into rivers
that'll soon be gone
Love it like fog
loves the ocean
its mother and bride
Dive so deep
past coral and kelp
past canyon and plain
into the abyss
where earth vents
its magnetic heart
so deep
you forget to come up
If you love it
really love it
don't just whisper its name

under the new moon
or light a candle
in the corner of your room
Don't give it
no golden bubbles
no silver spit
Love it so deep
the fist un-makes itself
as flower, and spring
forgets it was ever born
Love it all the way back to when
there weren't no lovers
and no love cuz baby
if you want to plant
your pelvis in this mud
be ready to let the lord
use your backbone
for a stake

Elisabeth Adwin Edwards

ODE TO IRON

Call me *Stellar Demise*, my hemoglobin pulses with the last exhalations
of stars. I have cast myself

into a cup, a scaffold, a fence, a pipe, a cup. That which is foundational,
marks the edge of a loving space, or fills

to overflowing, that which can be used as weapon, but more often
the thing that spills

over. Well-seasoned skillet, molasses, rust. Some days I'm so hard,
heavy. Others, so magnetic I can't move. I have carried water

no one would want to drink, water not fit for a child to bathe in.
Cells of the fetus I aborted at age twenty-one

bored through the blood-brain barrier and his tiny double-helixes
corkscrewed my mind. He still courses

through me. I imagine his eyes the color of black ore, like his father's.
Sometimes I dream him into a strong body, a body

outside of myself, a body I can touch, and I become a spigot, all I do is
weep. Another star died and found its way here.

Jeremy Radin

BEAUTIFUL

I am going to die alone, surrounded by beautiful women.
I am being very specific when I say beautiful, I mean
a casting of the eye elsewhere, is that what I mean? Sure.
Beautiful women, beautiful, let's forget me with each other.
One slept with me in order to "research a role."
One sucked upon my earlobe on the tram back
to the Eeyore section of the Disneyland parking lot.
It is patriotic to hurt each other & I am through
with patriotism. From now on, only time
is to be shattered by the promises breaking
all over it. I was promised a girl & a garden.
I waited. I became something else. You should
have seen me. I was so beautiful. I was so
fucking beautiful no one saw.

Clive Matson

SKULL CAVE
(Near Yubay, Baja California Sur)

The mammoth rock is hollowed out
as a skull's chamber. One eye hole,
half shut, bends shadows through the air.
The other is a smooth round frame

to rugged peaks, pale sky, and clouds.
The right ear is cocked into stone,
the left a narrow slit that flares
open on a green, sloping plane.

Birds feed on small insects that cruise
the chamber. Droppings smear the nose,
a v-shaped stone, below their perch.

A visitor may choose the view.
There's room to walk around the floor,
top of a spine set deep in earth.

Kathryn De Lancellotti

ROOT

Moonlight in the kitchen is a sign of God
—Anne Carson

A redwood falling is a sign of God,

is a boy who discovers
his father's homeless,

wants to feed every
hungry mouth

on every hungry corner.
A tree feeding its sapling

to reduce root competition
for the next generation

is a sign of God.
When a redwood

fell across Cold Springs Ct.
and blocked the road

to Planned Parenthood,
a woman listened—

she was stuck in a storm
and it took days to slice

the trunk away.
Two days too late

is a sign.
Is a dying tree

sending wisdom to its kin,
sending carbon

signals for defense.
The forest,

not a tangled mess
of competition—

but a mother reaching
for a star, rooting

into darkness
is a sign of God,

is wet soil,
that final place—

God's mouth
just waitingto swallow.

Bob Branaman

AN AFTERNOON PAINTING

Sometimes it just flows effortlessly.
Today I felt I was pushing it
Uphill.
Had something in mind
Based on the last few days of work
Of what I wanted or expected to get.
Pretty much unsatisfied
Till I gave up completely.
Started cleaning my brushes,
Then saw I didn't care anymore;
It was already a failure.
I got back into it,
Dripped a few things and let it be.

Now, sitting in the back yard
Watching the flowers and butterflies
Sway in the wind.

E.K. Keith

TEMPUS FUGIT

My alternate realities
are fantasizing
about time travel
as a weekend getaway

Take in a double feature
in an old Art Deco theater
with crushed red velvet seats
that spring up
when you stand

and sticky floors

Everything on screen
is the Golden Age
that never was

Stories fragmented
frame by frame

Nothing but light
in love with its own hype

My alternate realities
are fantasizing
about a future
where we figure out
how to feed everybody
and how everybody
has a place to live
because we've changed
our minds
and we can see
that the abundant earth
can still hold us all

because we know
what is shared
won't ever be wasted
or exploited

I'm traveling forward in time
through space

I have no control
over this   only
the work of my own hands
making reality

I'm traveling forward in time
in my mind
a kind of time machine

Imagination
takes me back
and pushes me forward

Imaginable futures
waiting for action

But let's not get ahead of ourselves

It's the little things
that count the most

Regular habits
like not buying paper towels
and food wrapped in plastic

Simple actions
make an imaginable future
possible

Don't wait

Leave dystopia
behind

Aruni Wijesinghe

WHEN BROWN BODIES MAKE THE NEWS

they are extras in a Duran Duran music video,
natives included in the shoot to lend local color.
This faraway place enters our collective consciousness
and we muse about going there someday
to loll on white beaches while sarong-d boys
bring us drinks decorated with hibiscus flowers.

When brown bodies make the news
our eyes flit over stories of civil wars
and suicide bombers. We can't believe
the kinds of atrocities that happen
over there, far away from sanitized studios
where we practice yoga. We press our palms
together in co-opted *namaste*, roll up our mats,
feel somehow enlightened.

When brown bodies make the news
we think how sad it is to see so many bodies
washed up on such beautiful beaches. We Google
"how to know if a tsunami is coming"
and learn to seek higher ground,
unlike those poor local fishermen, their huts flattened,
their children devoured by the sea. We surf
past these grim images in search of uplifting stories
of tourists who survive the wave and return
home to whole, dry houses.

When brown bodies make the news
they are pawns in tragedy, studded with shrapnel.
They are anonymous, not related to parents
or cousins or communities. We pause
to read news stories because the tragedy
is on Easter Sunday, a pastel day. We scan
the reports and count how many Americans
and Europeans are affected, consume details
about how lucky these pale bodies are to escape
disaster, how much those who are lost will be missed.

When brown bodies make the news, we are
just bodies. There are plenty more
where we came from. Tomorrow's news
will wash us away. Water sluices
across a scarred church, rinses away
the blood, the vivid of red against brown diluted.

Kevin Ridgeway

SOCIAL DISTANCE

I have no children,
am divorced
and I've got
a dead girlfriend.
I do not go to parties
because they all ask me
why I have no job,
and why I have no kids
and please don't make them
feel uncomfortable
before they are drunk
enough to act like
they are listening
when I discuss
my mental illness
and the fact
that I'm a fair weather
friend of Bill W.,
which spoils their fun
so I don't go
to parties anymore
because I am
too afraid I will
want to throw
a one-man party
beyond midnight
while they all sleep,
safe and sound
and unaware
of the sinister side
of me lurking among
shadow demons
in search of a light
that will lead me
back to them

before they all
wake up and notice
that I've been gone.

Iris Berry

FERAL LIKE ME
(for Lola the cat)

I think about you
and how much
we're alike
both left for dead
on streets,
too angry
and brutal
with people
that have love
on their lips
and blood lust
in their eyes
hearts
souls
and groins
as they dangle
the carrot
and say
here kitty, kitty.
I look at you
and think
how much
we're alike
both left for dead
on streets littered
with venom
vacant of empathy
and painted
with empty promises
at the intersections
of fuck you
and fuck me.
Intersections
that devour souls

at a mere whisper
and the hearsay
of love
vulnerability
honesty
and the scent
of kindness.
I look at you
and think
how much
we're alike
we were both
left for dead
by the very ones
that gave us life.
I know
I saved you
as you were being
swallowed
by a quicksand
of leaves
an old tire
a carburetor
and houses
foreclosed
out there
in the avenues
and the streets
where souls
go to die
and the last things
that come
the closest
to touching
their unwanted bodies
are chalk
and tape
for protection
that came
just a little too late.
I look at you

as you lay beside me
I feel warm
knowing
I saved you
and you
saved me.
I put my hand out
to touch your face
and you bite me
and then you lick
as if to apologize
for your nature
your instinct
and I let you
as I know
you only
do it
because
you're feral
like me
and I love you for it
all the more...

Kenneth Patchen

BUT OF LIFE

What I want in heart
—O stiller, wider, nearer—
Said the tree
Is that none come touching
For their own stuff

Any part of me
And over him a wall
of shifting fog began
To build, little on little—

Like a wet shroud.

No birds
Came then. And with them
Stars
Stayed. His poor branches
Trailed white and still. He
Wept. His loudest cry went unheard

So was Crucifixion's tree.

Jim Morrison

DRY WATER

As to the drowning man
hoarse whisper
invokes, on the edge,
an arroyo
Sangre de Christo

Violence in a time of plenty

There is one deaf witness
on the bank, the shore
leaning in finery against
a ruined wall
as Jesus did. Red livid lips,
pale flesh withdrawn from
ragged dress, pit of the past
& secrets unveiled in the
scarred chalk wall

When, often, one is not deluged
by rain, 3 drops suffice
The war is over there
I am neither doctor nor saint
Christ or soldier
Now, friends, don't look at me
sadly ranting like some
incomprehensible child
I know by my breath of what
I speak, & what I've seen
needs telling.
Please, freeze!
Danger near.
A message has started its path
to the heart of the brain
A thin signal is on its way
An arrow of hope, predicting rain
A death-rod bearing pain

Johnette Napolitano

EXQUISITE CORPSES

Exquisite Corpses
So we shall be
Delicate, skeletal
Poetry
Shriveling noses
and dry crumbling brains
Sifting to powder
like the finest cocaine

Exquisite Corpses
None so fine
 Breathless perfection
'til the end of time
Gracefully elegant in perfect repose,
as still and crisp
as a dry dead rose.

Breathtaking specimens
So we shall be
In caskets of mirrors
with no eyes to see
Your beautiful bones
now but sweet souvenirs.
No lips to whisper
No ears to hear

Rich Ferguson

WHEN CALLED IN FOR QUESTIONING

When asked about the scars around your lips,
tell them you were speaking peace in a shattered-glass world.

When asked about employment,
say you are a wound collector on the broken frontier.

As for where you reside,
tell them your heart is equidistant from joy & suffering,

the now & never,
the sweet flower & the Hiroshima cloud.

Regarding why you say the things you say,
tell them the full moon is in your mouth.

When asked about the ghosts behind your eyes,
say you occasionally spend too much time thinking

about who you are to become,
rather than whom you are supposed to be.

As for why some leave the world too soon,
tell them death's reflexes are sometimes quicker than prayer.

John Brantingham

WITH COLTRANE ON THE GREAT WESTERN DIVIDE

coltrane starts playing in my head
as i cross over the falls
coming off precipice lake

up here too high even for frogs
and no trees and nothing that moves
that i can see except

for the little saffron spiral bugs
who live in this water
that fades from clear to blue to green

and coltrane's blowing in my head
as the winds are blowing in my ears
and i can barely breathe up here

so my early morning trot
up this mountain is down to a plod
and i climb out of the bowl of lake

and up the other side
up to this place called kaweah gap
this low spot on the great western divide

and look on one side at the paternoster lake
i've just climbed out of
and on the other down at the broad arroyo

down at those little rings of foxtail pines
here and there scattered on a world
of brown grass until they reach

into the lodgepole forest
somewhere a mile below me
and then i realize what's been playing

through my head all this morning
and coltrane's there singing to me alone
because i'm the only one

in this wide world except
for those little buddhist monk bugs
dancing to his sax

in the water
and he's singing
that part of the song

a love supreme
a love supreme
a love supreme

over and over and he's right
and i know just exactly
what he means

Conney Williams

THE RAREST OF SIGHTINGS

when the last time
you see a man with no hands
claiming he's lonely

surrendered reason
for his heart to tender and daily
complaining he's hungry

this is how
living escapes the grasp
time mocks like a feral enemy

calculated wars
are fought over correctness
inject poison into opportunity

when the first time
you see a man take off his pride
pray before eats

he doesn't require
a god to repent or forgive
sacrifice always louder than bleats

do you see
a Black man when melanin
makes him invisible

birth certificate says
violent is the first name
last name is criminal

have you ever
trained with a Black man
trying to outrun racial profile

everyday he laments
the weight of his birthmark
whose premature death is not a disguise

Cecilia Woloch

FOR THE BIRDS: A CHARM OF GOLDFINCHES

Stopped under a sycamore, looked up:
bare white limbs against blue, blue sky
and in those branches, flickering, birds,
each with a pale green-yellow breast,
each the size of a small child's fist.
What kind of birds are you? I asked

and put on my glasses, the better to glimpse
such wing and color, such flashiness.
Then breathless climbed the sun-swept hill
to the visitor's center, rushed inside,
saying, "I have a question about a bird!"
Was given a book of birds to check.

Considered *Common Yellow Throat:*
Skulks in marshes.
Male wears black mask.
Wichity-wichity song
Loved that music, but maybe I'm wrong?

Was told that American Goldfinches turn
from winter's muddy greenish-brown
to summer's yellow brightness, turn
betwixt, in spring, this lemon-lime;
and fly *in hiccups,* flash their gold, a flock
of such birds called *a charm,*
from the Latin *carmen,* meaning *song.*

Ran back down the hill like a woman afire
practically into the sycamore's arms,
singing, anyway, *skulks in marshes,*
black mask, wichity-wichity song!
Singing, *Spread out your colors, oh flash me your wings*
as the charm made its green-yellow sweep through the sky

Daniel Yaryan

WE'RE FAR BELOW THE DARK SHROUD NIGHTS

So many signals lost
in the dark shroud nights

Antennae await

In the dark shroud nights

Cardiac heavyweights

Dark shroud nights

Point of liftoff debate

Dark shroud nights

Seek the cosmic gate

Dark shroud nights

Love lights flicker fate
Oh, you say humanity is at stake?

Signals lost
in the dark shroud nights

Inhabitants either make or break

In the dark shroud nights

While time freezes -- take, take, take
Greedy fakers of warmth
Fake you!
Fake you, so much!
Take you...
for so much!

Dark shroud nights

Power flux inequity...
claimstaker sweepstakes

So many signals lost
in the dark shroud nights

Beanstalk stalkers
climb down
rake up all the magic
and state, " I smell the blood
of an impoverished man."

All signals lost
in the dark shroud nights

Searching for strange new worlds
ego boosts from Cape Canaveral
publicity talkers of a forgotten planet

Left to the dark shroud nights...
Dark shroud nights

Hijackers of awareness
hiders of the compass
hinderers of our map back
to a home

Far
below
So far...
below

We're far
Below
the
Dark
Shroud
Nights

Laure-Anne Bosselaar

LE SOLEIL & LA LUNE

Look at that moon: she's all off-
      kilter & veiled & moody again tonight.

    Yet how all of Antwerp glowed with her
when I was seventeen! I was free, I had a lover, he lived hours
away – we wrote poems to each other every day —

      he had never loved as he loved me,
he discovered *le soleil et la lune* in my voice:

         La nuit, ta voix se mêle au clair de lune,
         Au calme clair de lune triste et beau,
         Qui fait rêver les oiseaux dans les arbres
         Et sangloter d'extase les jets d'eau…

    & I believed him, & he believed it too.

          He had stolen those lines
from Verlaine, I know that now — but so what? For months,
    in Flanders' moonlit streets, cafés & motel sheets,
      I was *le soleil* & I was *la lune*.

You know what happened. It could be
      the story of your first love too: it didn't last.
He left for the army overseas,
      and I for the mold & dust of libraries.
But here's the point: may I say it again?

    I was seventeen
        & for months, in Flanders' moonlit streets,
    cafés & motel sheets,
          I was *le soleil* & I was *la lune*.

Ellen Bass

THE SMALL COUNTRY

Unique, I think, is the Scottish *tartle*, that hesitation
when introducing someone whose name you've forgotten.

And what could capture *cafuné*, the Brazilian Portuguese way to say
running your fingers, tenderly, through someone's hair?

Is there a term in any tongue for choosing to be happy?

And where is speech for the block of ice
we pack in the sawdust of
    our hearts?

What appellation approaches the smell of apricots thickening the air
when you boil jam in early summer?

What words reach the way I touched you last night—
as though I had never known a woman—an explorer,
wholly curious to discover each particular
fold and hollow, without guide,
not even the mirror of my own body.

Last night you told me you liked my eyebrows.
You said you never really noticed them before.
What is the word that fuses this freshness
with the pity of having missed it.

And how even touch itself cannot mean the same to both of us,
even in this small country of our bed,
even in this language with only two native speakers.

A. Razor

ON THE DESERT WIND THIS MORNING

when you've cheated death
so many times,
death finally
tries to cheat you back

is it a crime?
to give away
the ending
over & over
until nothing
seems surprising

guns pointed at my head
I can't really call it
you got your trigger finger ready
you gonna pull it?
I know you'd like to
with your new flag
that only shows blue

how far apart have we become?
seems like a chasm larger than
the world we were supposed to
share
but since there is no history of that
then tell your story
blaring thru the loudspeakers
clogging all the broadcast airwaves
live-streaming your death threats
as the death rains down
then seeps up from below ground

it seems like a few wanted to lead
the multitudes
to a hallowed ground of
overnight delivery
where the earth beneath our feet
could be scorched from
an anonymous space
      above us

those left in the wreckage cry out
for the murdered part of our
fellowship
    those who would want
to just
clean us up
throw us out
like the garbage
they perceive us to be
those are the ones
who clamor for
     the guns
to them
this will always
     be
the Wild West
with a silent movie
dramatic history
    where they always
    win
     no matter what
no job too dirty
for their overwhelming
     calvary
coming to their rescue
so they can continue
their pillage & rape
without regard
     to where their wealth
    originated
as the wind
blows the

sound of
the last
bugle
before
the last
charge begins
& the report of
the guns blazing
drowns out the screams
of the last children
of the last people
who called the desert home
just to try to get away from
the pillars of progress
that tower over all this
imminent domain
they paid for
with our blood

Dion O'Reilly

PEACOCK

All Leif's punk friends hated me
with my mullet and sellout job.
No skin-tight glamor, no heroine pallor,
I followed his band around Seattle
like an orphan follows a stand-in dad,
prayed a wave of energy might
pass through him, a God particle
oscillate his bones enough to feel me.

But then, Oh victory! He took a walk with me—
the night, full of wind, a storm
lifting water from Lake Washington
like it might become sky and drown us.

He wrapped me in his arms,
said I was his girlfriend,
drove me home on his motorcycle.
To his bed! Then fell asleep
without touching me.
And so it went for many years.

There's more to the story,
but I like best how much I craved him.
Second best, how much I hated him
when he took a second woman.
I like to remember my fevered jealousy
when he stole my peacock feathers,
gifted them to her like a bouquet,
how he let me smell her perfume
on his sweater, watched me
scream my dirtiest epithets
as he fingered his guitar.

It was forty years ago my anger tore
like a fire break against a greater flame.
I like to think I'll never
burn like that again. But I could.

It's never too late to believe
a beautiful story, start a war
to keep it true.

Holly Prado

FOR POETS IN AUTUMN

roses become their concentrated shells
carriers of seed

lorca neruda akhmatova
the dead we see the dead who see us
in this country where nothing ends

the birthmark on all our mouths
the slow mirror a bond

why go on except for such a family

Jamie Asaye FitzGerald

TULIPS UNBOUND

Tulips turn their faces to the sun
like people on a cold day.

One flower presses its head
against the window's latch.

It wants to push itself
into the daylit world.

I wish for the window
to spring open like a flower,

for the tulips would surely
lift from the vase,

flutter vermillion petals,
flap green-winged leaves,

and soar over L.A.
like a flock of wild parrots.

Kelly Gray

THE INVERSE HISTORY OF SPILLED MOUTH

To be sure, there is no history for me. No map
leading backwards to origin, just a closet
in suburbia where we erase and erase till the paint chips

to reveal

a scoured white spot and out of my mouth falls
a book with my tongue on a page. Cling lapping to ink,
a squid in open space in the upside-down world of

under the sheets, grabbing what I cannot see.

Still, the point is: my birth goes unremembered.
No childhood familiars, only a tree I pretend
into creature form between my legs, hot with running

breath in nostrils,   gallop lullaby,

school bus rides marked with incantations,
rise and ride, come great horse, resurrect your golden
haunches as good as any lunch bag shared. I escape

on your back, you wild oak with mane of leaves and burl.

Riding. Later, I point to pullouts along backroads
where hotrods became bridled, because as orphans
we are always called upon to nurse our way back home,

hungry babies looking for wheat to press our faces into.

Even if I collect all the bones from a field
like a good child, naming birds after dead naturalists
who ravish war fields, making hives of taxonomy,

collecting decapitated (yes, collecting is the root of *not yours*)

bodies as I go, perhaps delicately, perhaps not,
I still know that every battle has a border, (&)
even if I amass the bones,

I am Place, borderless.

Burrowless, I climb trees in the fog banks, sly tailed,
sky eyed. It takes a certain savvy to hang
the clavicles of squirrels from limbs,

all that climbing with things in your mouth.

Make a list titled Ways to Mark Territory:
scream throw rocks piss in circles, *this is mine*, arm cut
girl knife steal eggs yelping open your mouth to expose

the hole to your insides that is your only birthright,
tonsiled and lipstretched,

you can ask anyone who lives in the woods what does a wild
animal sound like at night~ and the answer is always,
always, a woman screaming.

Harry E. Northup

POETRY IS A PRAYER

A spontaneous prayer
An emotion, image, or images,
Words put together
In a clean, condensed way

A line as strict & free
As the Soul Train line
With ellipses, hyphens,
With no summation

Light with shadows
Love, gratitude, remorse,
Brokenness, patches
Sewn togeter by getting

Out of the way
Of the wind through barbed wire
With grandmother's (maternal) gentleness
& grandfather's (paternal) harshness

A breath with no beginning
No water pouring
Only gratitude, receptiveness
Flame of sky, open door

7 14 21

Judith Ayn Bernhard

WILL THE POETS KEEP QUIET?

No.
They will not.
They will not linger in the gloaming they will not idle in the daybreak they
will not drowse at noon.

The poets will speak.
They will whisper to their lovers they will talk among themselves they will
relate and orate and berate.

They will traverse to converse and scramble to gabble.

They will stop and chat about this and that they will discuss what is old hat
they will rhyme and keep time.

The poets will speak.
They will scurry to the dais they will lean upon the lectern they will hold
forth in the hall.

They will hit and miss and flail and fail they will proclaim and declaim and
defame and inflame.

The poets will pounce to pronounce they will praise and amaze they will
search their souls for days.

The poets will not keep quiet.
The poets will speak.

Lewis MacAdams

THE VOICE OF THE RIVER

                is a red wing blackbird
twittering in the trash bags
  festooned across the
    branches of a cottonwood
      like prayer flags.

The freeways are louder than the River.
    The I-5, the 110, the L.B.
      overwhelm the River and its tributaries
        with their roar. But when the tributaries
          bring their gifts of rain water to the main stem

the River can be louder than
     the thunder rolling out of the San Gabriels.
         The Voice of the River
is the golf balls clanking in the
power towers, and the kids on their bicycles
laughing when they spot the mud people
      moving along the sand bars
        in silent meditation.

I hear the River singing through the passing railroad cars,
    the screeching metal as a Metrolink commuter train
      tears apart. News choppers circle overhead, the howling
        ambulance sirens
          followed by the coyote pack's howl.

The high-pitched chi and the endless meetings,
                always one or two more,
  the laptops clicking, the TMDL's,
    the BMP's, the RFP's, the SSO's and
      the UAA's; the murmuring bureaucrats, the sharp
              whack of gavels,
  the deep voice of command,
    the swooping bats and the swallows and swifts—

  I listen for them to make my own hearing more acute—
    the scream of a fishhawk, the flapping of a hundred pigeons,
    and the rock doves too scatter in fear,
        a Great Blue Heron's
    sorrowful honk, the trill and ripple of water
      moving across rocks.
          At the center of itself
 the River is silence,
  and that's where I come in:
   with the sounds in my head
     and the words in my heart.

Lew Welch

SONG OF THE TURKEY BUZZARD

                                            For Rock Scully   *who*
heard it
                                            the first
                                            time

Praises, Tamalpais,
    Perfect in Wisdom and Beauty,
She of the Wheeling Birds
                                  I.

The rider riddle is easy to ask,
but the answer might surprise you.
How desperately I wanted Cougar
(I, Leo, etc.)
            brilliant proofs: terrain,
color, food, all
nonsense. All made up.
                        They were always there, the
           laziest high-flyers, bronze-winged,
                          the silent ones
         "A cunning man always laughs and smiles,
                even if he's desperately hungry,
        while a good bird always flies like a vulture,
                  even if it is starving."
                (Milarepa sang)

Over and over again, that sign:

I hit one once, with a .22
heard the "flak" and a feather flew off, he
flapped his wings just once and
went on sailing. Bronze
(when seen from above)
                      as I have seen them, all day sitting
                      on a cliff so steep they
                      circled below me, in the up-draft
                      passed so close I could see his
                      eye.

Praises Tamalpais,
  Perfect in Wisdom and Beauty,
She of the Wheeling Birds

Another time the vision was so clear another saw it, too. Wet, a hatching bird, the shell of the egg streaked with dry scum, exhausted, wet, too weak to move the shriveled wings, fierce sun-heat, sand. Twitching, as with elbows (we all have the same parts). Beak open, neck stretched, gasping for air. O how we want to live!
"Poor little bird," she said, "he'll never make it."

Praises, Tamalpais,
  Perfect in Wisdom & Beauty,
She of the Wheeling Birds

Even so, I didn't get it for a long long while. It finally came in a trance, a coma, half in sleep and half in fever-mind. A Turkey Buzzard, wounded, found by a rock on the mountain. He wanted to die alone. I had never seen one, wild, so close. When I reached out, he sidled away, head drooping, as dizzy as I was. I put my hands on his wing-shoulders and lifted him. He tried, feebly, to tear at my hands with his beak. He tore my flesh too slightly to make any difference. Then he tried to heave his great wings. Weak as he was, I could barely hold him.

A drunken veterinarian found a festering bullet in his side, a .22 that slid between the great bronze scales his feathers were. We removed it and cleansed the wound.

Finally he ate the rotten gophers I trapped and prepared for him. Even at first, he drank a lot of water. My dog seemed frightened of him.

> They smell sweet
>   meat is dry on their talons
> The very opposite of
>   death
> bird of re-birth
>   Buzzard
> meat is rotten meat made

          sweet again and
     lean, unkillable, wing-locked
        soarer till he's but a
    speck in the highest sky
    eye finds Feast! on
        baked concrete
free!
    squashed rabbit ripened:
       our good cheese
(to keep the highways clean, and bother no Being)

              II.
        Praises Gentle Tamalpais
   Perfect in Wisdom and Beauty of the
           sweetest water
       and the soaring birds
   great seas at the feet of thy cliffs

Hear my last Will & Testament:

    Among my friends there shall always be
    one with proper instructions
    for my continuance.

        Let no one grieve.
        l shall have used it all up
        used up every bit of it.

        What an extravagance!
        What a relief!

On a marked rock, following his orders,
place my meat.

        All care must be taken not to
        frighten the natives of this
        barbarous land, who
        will not let us die, even,
        as we wish.

With proper ceremony disembowel what I
no longer need, that it might more quickly
rot and tempt

my new form

* * *

NOT THE BRONZE CASKET BUT THE BRAZEN WING

SOARING FOREVER ABOVE THEE O PERFECT

O SWEETEST WATER O GLORIOUS

WHEELING

BIRD

RD Armstrong

JACK'S ADVICE
Take care of your teeth and your asshole.
— Jack Micheline

a chance encounter with the poet Jack Micheline
outside of a north hollywood book store
yielded this gem
too old to be wide-eyed I was
leaning into a wall
ever the outsider
hanging back
when up he walked with a couple of dudes
poets I guess (they have a certain swagger)
and someone asks him for "life" advice and
Jack says what he says

I wish I had taken it to heart
especially while the Dentist is
pulling rotten teeth out of my head

I won't even talk about
what's going on with my asshole

Jack Micheline

I AM A POET

I am a poet
I am an angel
I am a thief
I am a beggar
I write poems with blood
my head seems heavy now
I am able to laugh
I am able to cry
I am serious about life
I am frantic about life
I live in a very immediate state
I cannot earn a living
I go on the streets and beg for money
because money makes one rotten
because money buys eggs
because money is what everybody asks for
because money has driven me mad

I am a poet
I am a beggar
I am a thief
I live like the lowest form of all life
I am a real poet and that is rare
yet people run away from the real
yet people's faces I see are very sad
because they always want more
because they are not happy
because they think security is life
because they think they are realists
because they think they are practical
like business men are practical

I have touched the leaves of trees
I have seen a field of wheat in the grass
I have seen light in the darkest night
I have felt the air of poetry
I have remembered one sentence
that cannot be taught at any university of learning
that was the key to my life
I have run wild in streets
I have died many times
I have been by the rocky shores

this world I live in kills poets
this world I live in is insane
this life that I live is real
I am a poet
I am a real poet
I beg for money in the streets like a dog
like the lowest animal

death is always alone
death is lonely and sad
death is misery
death always seeks more misery
death denies their own death
death denies all living things
death has the power to defy death
death is unable to love
death is enclosed in bank vaults
death is fear and armaments
death is taught at universities
death has never loved
because fear teaches at the university of all learning

I am a poet
I am an angel
I am a thief
I am a beggar
love will save us
love will defy death
love will cut the bonds of birth

I read my poems to the moon and howl
I sit down on the curb and cry and defy all madness
I defy the murderers of all living life
I defy the madness of all civilization

I am a poet
I am a thief
I am an angel
I am a beggar
I write poems with my blood
my head seems heavy now
I shall go on the streets
and beg for money
like the lowest animal

Jessica Loos

GOALS
for Gregory Corso

Sicilian cell block pacer
habit never lost after doin' time
for elevatin' crime
to a scientific level
through the use of lookout walkie talk
whenever someone said Allen Ginsberg
he'd shout: over n' out
that mutha fucker better not
outlive me

Stuart Z. Perkoff

UNTITLED

poets of the world, be
    careful. i can't say it
strongly
enuf. i know
i know
i tell you i know
that she stands on every street corner waiting & watching
that she looks into the dark doorways & empty windows seeking
that she tirelessly walks up & down the hard streets of our world
calling

   watch out, you fools. you are blind
as well as deaf. that's one of the things she hates.
be careful, poets.
its not enuf
to put a pretty word
next to another one.
a real image or two
studding yr verse
wont save you at this reckoning.
this is the real
thing. take
cover, poets.
she is knocking on the door
are you shivering in yr shit filled shoes?
have you roses growing out of yr nostrils?
she is coming
she is coming
she is coming thru the door
she is coming up the stairs
she is opening the doors of the bedrooms & the eyes, looking in
she wants to hear no stories
she wants to hear no songs.
i think she's had her belly full of singing.

she is merciless.
she knows what you have done
there is no use crying abt it, making up fancy tales
you've gotten too good at that
anyway.
   she'll take it back. it's hers. she wants it back.
run poets, run.
hide poets, hide.
be careful
take cover
i warn you
i know. i tell you, this i know.
she's coming. up & down the streets, in & out of the houses, in the
   dark & the lite, seeking, looking, crying, mercilessly
   examining every dark soul.
i warn you
she is as relentless as you wd expect her
to be.
it's hers. you know it. when she finds you
she will take it back.

Wanda Coleman

O SOUL CONCEALED BELOW

i dance the snake—a torturous samba

bramble-haired, wine-eyed, skin seared
wailing against the cave against the tower
stinking of poverty, of burnt rubber and water-based
paint, patchouli oil and sage, gasoline and auto
exhaust, stinking to high hell

all verticals within the horizontals, ventricles
overworked. called Quasheba but lived life without
Sundays—a severity of tongues, a raw vernacular
the freight of jealousies a cloak of hornets, on my way
nowhere, voiceless, unheard, yet seeking redress

glide under glide the sweet spring sun forgotten
gods cavorting the thought horizon, recreating the moon full-
splendor

heartbeats, slumber's depths—the music of moans

swells of air/eternity unraveling becoming the length of time
it takes to capture his attention. at ecstasy's gate
i am the fat woman scratching her breast in public, arm—heavy
like a tired swimmer, yet stitching together my garment
of sunlight and sand/crossing the ninth boundary
to a field of white crosses, salvation defied

in last night's dream i searched the bed sheets
and one-by-one removed the slender knives from
the folds, those lovely long thin knives with serrated blades

he places himself beneath me that I may grasp and climb
his body—first the altar then prey then the offering—
as i am transformed, from calm to cunning,
from logy to lusty, from wife to wanton/our ritual before
couplings as we snake and coil, one across the other

skin against skin, flame into flame

> *and the dark shineth in the light*
> *and the lightness comprehended it not*

Douglas Kearney

HEADNOTE TO A DONE POEM
For Wanda Coleman

Dear L.A.,
I am sorry for your—Dear

Baja and Bay, I am sorry
for your—Dear Jagged West,
I am sorry for

your—Dear Aged East,
I am sorry for your—Dear Shine

to Seas, I am sorry for

your—Dear Pole to Pole, I am
sorry for your—Dear Ice
and Soil, I am sorry

for your—Dear Ear Canaled, I

am sorry for your—Dear Eyeballed,
I am sorry for your—Dear Tongued

and Dear Thumbed, I am

sorry for your—Dear Nostrilled,
oh my dear Nostrilled, I am sorry for your loss,
your loss of the funk, your funkless,
bereft loss of that gut bucket busting
with Birds of Paradise, church socks,
with coffee grounds and soggy paperbacks.

whiffs of ziplocked poppies and pissways,
boocoo tail pipes belting yellow notes and backfire.
ramschackled passels of green apples under underpasses.
oil paints gone fungal under summer sun.

of kerosene, the rainbow in the Valvoline pool
and the bronzed coin slicked gold down there.

Dear South L.A.,
I am sorry for your loss of Central,
ghost now, ganked and gaffled,
cuffed and trunked with stuff we knew
and stuff we don't, stuff we was meant to get,
to hold to, but butterfingered, let slip.
stuff we figured we'd catch next time round,
but it was Sunday at midnight at a bus stop, Watts—
and the street gone dark for going mute.

Dear Salt Petered 110,
Dear Weird Skied 10,
Dear Mortared 405,
Dear Spider Legged 5,
Dear Wheezing 14,
I regret your riverboat queenlessness,
the white-walled paddlewheel moored in the dock.
gnash and chomp over this new dry-spell,
holler for your tarred beds and stiff necks.

Dear Soap Operas and Soapboxes,
I am sorry for your— Dear
Chitins and Chitlins, I am sorry for
your—Dear Pink Slips and Slipper Print,
I am sorry for your—

Dear Civic Offices of Wrung Hands and Ringing Lines,
I regret to be informed of this new Earthquake cure.
that our smogscrapers won't come to shiver
with pleasure, with terror, with snits.
I regret the asphalt won't fault to black cracks
jabbing down to Earth's orange heart,
Dear Crust, Dear Mantle. sorry no bell will
toll us below our tables. Dear Formica,
Dear Veneer, I'm sorry we won't peer
beneath you and find hard fists of Bubblicious.

Dear Mouthful of Oysters and Seeds, I am
sorry for your—Dear Mouthful of Pop Bottles,
I am sorry for your—Dear Mouthful
of 45s and Candy Hearts,
I regret you must peck bread at a stranger's park bench,
peck bread out a new bag, sweet flock. a new pocket, hot damn.

Dear Throat of Grout, Throat of Fruit,
I regret the loss of low down loupsgarou,
of toe-holed nylon. a bushel of neon onions on a Zenith,
unpeeling. the peal of sand pelting corrugated steel, stolen.
the quiet storm that slumbers behind molars, pulled.
the daybreak bitten like a kumquat, puked.
the slow drag's sloe wound, the rag's ragged, sink-bound flight.
the alley's gold teeth. the floor fan's hum as it rumbles with July.

Dear Amnesiac Eardrums,
I am—forget it.
Dear Channel Surfing No-see-ums,
I am—never mind.
Dear Ruffled Hatchlings,
I am sorry for your pinions, your guano tinted lenses,
for your shook-assery at tremors, and your tattooed blacklists,
your little yellow tongues. I am sorry for big feet,
the Blue Parade, turned Blue Cortege, turned Second Line,
all the pages it left, all the papers that pile
your boulevard cobbled with eggshells.
Dear Armless Palm Trees,

I am sorry you could not catch her,
Dear Armless Palm Trees,

why couldn't you catch her?

Dear Children of the, of the—,
my great regret for reckoning you wouldn't want,
all what's left below folding chairs,
in garage-rotting boxes,
and by the final curb,
her words where her picture would be,
the picture where her words.
Dear What's Left of Us,
I regret we didn't know
a mind like a heart
was no mark-ass simile.
Dear Family
Dear Austin
Dear
I

Luis J. Rodriguez

PERHAPS

Perhaps when the stories are lost and pleasure is a dry river
and what makes the flesh sing is a long-gone supplication,
we may find our true names.

Perhaps when the earth's rotation stops, when the moon has wilted,
and the sun's rays scorch down this squandered ground,
we may uncover our inner eye.

Perhaps when the poisons that once were our sustenance
and the radiation that once gave us light, now foster
our insatiable hungers and an abiding darkness,
we may know what really feeds and guides us.

Perhaps after we've created so many borders, so many walls,
and conjured up even more laws to make even more lawless,
we may realize it's ourselves who've been made illegal,
it's our spirits we've alienized.

Perhaps when parents lose their final grasps on their children,
they will finally grasp that their sole purpose is to bring loved,
healthy,
and understood children into this world—to remake
the universe, better and more holy each time.

Perhaps when the wars in the names of countless gods,
which look and act like those who evoke them, finally end,
we may realize that God is the unnamable, unobtrusive wind
that caresses our cheeks, the rain that falls on us all,
the air that enters our lungs, and the nerves in our brains
so we can name whatever God we want.

Perhaps when all the textbooks and written histories
and science papers cease, we'll understand that nature,
and our own natures, are the source of all knowledge,
language, and histories, and we'll always be able to rewrite them,
reimagine them, and reweave them into the world.

Perhaps when love has become the embers of what we hate,
the residue of what we've destroyed, we'll know that love
is the stream that flows through each and every one of us,
the water we thirst for in the deserts of our days,
the ocean from which all our tears,
full of salt and unmet desires,
surge and flow.

Steve Abee

A LOVE POEM AND A POEM OF THANKS AND MEMORY TO MY WIFE

I use to have lots of things in my head.
All kinds of wild dominoes.
Now we live with the stones of truth.
One ain't better. They all the same.
All the same. Broken from the tree of meaning.
A sea awash in the cold now of never again.
It's there. You look close at what you're breathing.
You see the sunlight on your forehead.
Grab it.

I spoke sunsets in dirty parking lots of the 1990s.
I got the news of my grandmother's death right there.
Cars rushing by. The sun caught in haze.
It was smog love. It was Manson daughterhood.
It was alcoholic truth student. It was Yogananda tears.
It was sunlit psychology. Looking. Mind?
Find you in the Modelo.
She hugged me after.
When I was alone and my folks had left.
The news all over us.
We fell in sorrow's love pool.
There's no other explanation.
You held me when I had no guts anymore.
I was empty but my body wouldn't walk away.
I have tried to say thank you, so many times.
But the words aren't even words.
They are windows of light spoken in belly caves
On street corners, in sad smog light
3:30pm, Fall. 1993.

I used to have lots of things.
Now I have more
And they are simply oceanic.

Gary Snyder

NIGHT SONG OF THE LOS ANGELES BASIN

    Owl
     calls,
      pollen dust blows
Swirl of light strokes writhing
knot-tying light paths,

    calligraphy of cars.

Los Angeles basin and hill slopes
Checkered with streetways. Floral loops
Of the freeway express and exchange.

    Dragons of light in the dark
    sweep going both ways
    in the night city belly.
    The passage of light end to end and rebound,
    —ride drivers all heading somewhere—
    etch in their traces to night's eye-mind

    calligraphy of cars.

Vole paths. Mouse trails worn in
On meadow grass;
Winding pocket-gopher tunnels,
Marmot lookout rocks.
Houses with green watered gardens
Slip under the ghost of the dry chaparral,

    Ghost
    shrine to the L. A. River
    The jinja that never was there
    is there.
    Where the river debouches
    the place of the moment
    of trembling and gathering and giving

so that lizards clap hands there
—just lizards
come pray, saying
"please give us health and long life."

   A hawk,
   a mouse.

Slash of calligraphy of freeways of cars.

   Into the pools of the channelized river
   the Goddess in tall rain dress
   tosses a handful of meal.

   Gold bellies roil
   mouth-bubbles, frenzy of feeding,
   the common ones, the bright-colored rare ones
   show up, they tangle and tumble,
   godlings ride by in Rolls Royce
   wide-eyed in brokers' halls
   lifted in hotels
   being presented to, platters
   of tidbit and wine,
   snatch of fame,

      churn and roil,

   meal gone the water subsides.

   A mouse,
   a hawk.

The calligraphy of lights on the night
   freeways of Los Angeles

   will long be remembered.

   Owl
  calls;
    late-rising moon.

Phoebe MacAdams

EVEN BIRDS ARE COMPLICATED

Listen and translate the blessed entanglements,
says a voice in my dream,
like this green shawl, a gift from Roberta,
or the red throated hummingbirds
and the finches battling for food.

Will calls with news from Selkirk, New York,
the old family house.
He saw the barn wallboard
where my grandfather measured
the grandchildren each July fourth,
where he saw his twin brother's ghost,
and where he died.

This is about knots, words,
even birds are complicated

but about the shawl: in March
I walked into a room full of women knitting for God.
Are there any rules? I asked.
Three by five feet, they said, pray
and then give it away.

William J. Margolis

A (PROSE)POEM STRICTLY FOR THE LOCAL SCENE, LIKE, MAYBE IT'S AN OPEN LETTER TO HERBERT Q. CAEN

It starts this way: Dear Unadulterated Sir:
    It may no doubt come as a shock to you
    that the word <u>beat</u> comes from, well,
    let's face it, man, IS a four-letter
        anglo-saxon word.

It goes like this: Dear As-Yet-Unobliterated Sir:
    It may surprise you, but <u>beat</u> is, well
    one of those nasty-type Chaucer words,
    like, well, <u>love</u> and <u>care</u>: Two more signs
        the squares have turned inside-out.
Man, like, love is that feeling you get
when you think of, you know, that soap
and the skin you hope to touch...
while care comes in little packages, these days,
mass produced to alleviate
our neo-victorian jukebox refrigerator guilts.
        I mean,

It says to him: Dear Undesirable Sir:
    It may come as no surprise to you
    (though I'm sure you'd decently hide the fact)
    that there just aren't any of these "Beatniks"
    around here – at least everyone I've asked denies it.
        Like, man,
we know, we understand your problems, we dig that
you and all the other flatter-flacks
couldn't make your buck
if you didn't have a foil for the buttered side
of your bread – I mean, those well-breaded buddies
you bend the elbow with at those high places...

           Like, we dig,
we're your fall guys, the old dragon-at-the-gates
routine. The scapegoats you can put down, and out,
so your contented, moneyer-than-thou feeling
won't scrape on the bottom of our frayed & failing
faith in the great American Triple Play, I mean,
your confidence in the consecrated con-game of
        Profits, Progress & Pass the A-munition.

I say to the man: Dear UnAmerican Sir:
    When anybody says to me: 'Are you now,
or have you ever been, or was your great-grand-
twice-removed-third-cousin's-father-in-law's-
son or daughter ever a member
of the "Beat Generation?"' Why, man, I answer quick,
I say, like, uh, er, ah, that is... Huh?
Well... beat??? You mean...?
Well, I'll tell you:
           I was walking down Grant Avenue
the other night, floatin' kinda high, like,
you know, man, like my chick, she just,
well, she said I was the <u>most</u> to her
and she said she wanted to make it with me
like, <u>always</u>. Well, I was out of my skull
with stuff like that buzzin' my brain
and man, I didn't even <u>notice</u> these guys
gorilla suits – why I just didn't <u>see</u> them.
And when I pass by, they say: "There's one:
There's a weirdie! There's one of them Beatniks!"
And man, they came at me like
that leather jacket crowd
in their Brooks Brothers disguises,
and they grabbed my arms
and they grabbed my beard
and they had a ball, baby, all <u>over</u> me;
I mean I was for real what you'd call BEAT.
Like, I swear that by the time
the fuzz walked up and asked me if I was
        annoying these gentlemen
I was, have been ever since, and always will be
a genuine, life-dues-paid-up, scar-carrying member
      of the "Beaten-Up Generation" !

But this epistle to the Philistine does come to an end:

It says in brief: Dear Unspeakable Sir:
    Man, why don't you just forget all about
    this "Beat Generation" & "Beatnik" bullshit
    so, everybody else can, too.

    I mean, maybe then some of us poets, painters and all,
    who were never "beat" nor had time for such crap,
    and its flacks, maybe then we could do our work,
    make our buck, drink our wine,
    and not be pestered by stupid questions from
    stupid reporters and their square-but-vicarious-kick-
    seeking readers any more. I mean, like
        Bow Out, man.
                Cool it!

            later,
                    /s/ William J. Margolis

Fred Voss

THE EARTH AND THE STARS IN THE PALM OF OUR HAND

"Another day in paradise,"
a machinist says to me as he drops his time card into the time
clock and the sun
rises
over the San Gabriel mountains
and we laugh
it's a pretty good job we have
considering how tough it is out there in so many other factories
in this era of the busted union and the beaten-down worker
but paradise?
and we walk away toward our machines ready for another
10 hours inside tin walls
as outside perfect blue waves roll onto black sand Hawaiian beaches
and billionaires raise martini glasses
sailing their yachts to Cancun
but I can't help thinking
why not paradise
why not a job
where I feel like I did when I was 4
out in my father's garage
joyously shaving a block of wood in his vise with his plane
as a pile of sweet-smelling wood shavings rose at my feet
and my father smiled down at me and we held
the earth and the stars in the palm of our hand
why not a job
joyous as one of these poems I write
a job where each turn of a wrench
each ring of a hammer makes my soul sing out glad for each drop
of sweat
rolling down my back because the world has woken up and
stopped worshiping money
and power and fame
and because presidents and kings and professors and popes
and Buddhas and mystics

and watch repairmen and astrophysicists and waitresses
and undertakers know
there is nothing more important than the strong grip and
will of men

carving steel
like I do
nothing more important than Jorge muscling a drill through steel
plate so he can send money
to his mother and sister living under a sacred mountain in
Honduras
nothing more noble
than bread on the table and a steel cutter's grandson
reaching for the moon and men
dropping time cards into time clocks and stepping up to their
machines
like the sun
couldn't rise
without them.

Philip Levine

THEY FEED THEY LION

Out of burlap sacks, out of bearing butter,
Out of black bean and wet slate bread,
Out of the acids of rage, the candor of tar,
Out of creosote, gasoline, drive shafts, wooden dollies,
They Lion grow.
                      Out of the gray hills
Of industrial barns, out of rain, out of bus ride,
West Virginia to Kiss My Ass, out of buried aunties,
Mothers hardening like pounded stumps, out of stumps,
Out of the bones' need to sharpen and the muscles' to stretch,
They Lion grow.
                      Earth is eating trees, fence posts,
Gutted cars, earth is calling in her little ones,
"Come home, Come home!" From pig balls,
From the ferocity of pig driven to holiness,
From the furred ear and the full jowl come
The repose of the hung belly, from the purpose
They Lion grow.
                      From the sweet glues of the trotters
Come the sweet kinks of the fist, from the full flower
Of the hams the thorax of caves,
From "Bow Down" come "Rise Up,"
Come they Lion from the reeds of shovels,
The grained arm that pulls the hands,
They Lion grow.
                      From my five arms and all my hands,
From all my white sins forgiven, they feed,
From my car passing under the stars,
They Lion, from my children inherit,
From the oak turned to a wall, they Lion,
From they sack and they belly opened
And all that was hidden burning on the oil-stained earth
They feed they Lion and he comes.

Lynne Thompson

THE WAYS OF REMEMBERING WOMEN

I

Do you want to know about the *black dahlia* or
do you want the truth about Elizabeth Short?

You may not be aware: there is no such dahlia
and yet, lovers of crime focus on the dark of it,

the mystery connecting Miss Short to its rare
essence which, some say, means *enduring grace.*

I thought it was the newspapers who coined it,
eager to make a buck featuring the brutality of

that January, 1947, but no. It was the sailor men
who frequented the waterfront along the Long

Beach pier who gave the raven-haired Betty her
final moniker. They could have called her Rose

for the tattoo on her left calf; could have called
her Star for those who said she was an actress,

"well-behaved" and "sweet" despite the hideous
tableau she was found in—her head, torso, and

legs savagely detached, each from the other.
Her body drained of blood. Her mouth slashed

from one ear to the other. Her skull pulp-like as
it roiled in the tall grass of Leimert Park. Did you

know she was pregnant, her fetus removed post-mortem
by her killer? That a Chandler—yes, one

of *those* Chandlers—was rumored to be the daddy
and still, we can't get enough of her, of anything

that made her macabre. See: *Times* Magazine,
2015, describing many confessors to her murder,

every one looking for their mainline to notoriety.
See how, even now, you want to know *who* did it

as well as the horrific facts: the Dahlia was alive
when a butcher's knife scrolled calyx to corolla.

II

See how you don't remember just four years
before the Lady Dahlia there had been another

Betty, *neé* Nuñez, although there are reasons
that you forget. She was, it is said, a *pachuca*

who hung out along Sleepy Lagoon, listened to
Central Avenue jazz and junked old folks' tales

of docile Mexicanas, who sported plucked eye-brows,
darkened lips & an up-do held in place

by "rats". How many of you remember those
10 days in June, 1943? If not, re-read *News-*

week's piece not-so-subtly making judgments
about the "loose girls of LA's Mexican quarter";

indicting them as delinquents waylaying so-
called innocent service men with hip-swaying

& jitterbugging. "The girl-companions of zoot-
suiters" (so dubbed, whether it's true or not,

by the media and by whites) with their own
style. Many were just girls who were forced

to testify against friends or face detention,
or worse. Yet we only remember them, if we

recall them at all, as *mestizas*: cultural hybrids,
traitors, slaves, sell-outs; like many women

who came to L.A.—see: Nuñez and Short—
to find different identities and found them

as virgin or whore in someone's film or play,
or as the unremembered to the rest of us.

What can they ever say about what it is all
of us say about them? To paraphrase an old

African *until the lioness becomes historian,
some other animal will always tell her story.*

Luke Johnson

THE UNNAMED GARDEN

Here is where your daddy
thread a knife
through the mother deer's belly

and bellowed
when your fingers found

the fawn
and pulled it, wilted
from the body's cave, both eyes

widened and still.
Where once, on a walk,

when fog had crept
its muddy swill over the flash
of flood lights, you hid

your face afraid
the Lord would spit, his right hand

raised to strike.
You, half-nude, cock
still throbbing wet,

having joined a woman
twice your age

and tasted
where the womb began, its brine
the beauty of cream, bent

like one before a whip
to pay your filthy penance.

You bad boy dumb boy you
never enough boy, you fed
the body what it craved

and cowered by the climbing rose
that choked the wooden trellis.

How dare you.

Didn't you hear
the woman weep, while wandering
out to find you,

her voice
like something slick and fraught

sought for someplace
to drink, a body to wear, begged you
in from the cold?

You cradled the fawn.
You offered it back to the snow

and your daddy said *here*
by which he meant sip, to swallow
the moon's graffiti.

Sarah Maclay

SONG OF THE BROKEN DICE

It was then that I'd quit bathing—
then that I could no longer share my body
in the sleet or even along the rain-bathed diagonal
street that revealed a room for rent in the run-down mauve
of a Norman French façade (its jutting helmet),
then I'd wave, instead, to the lone Salvadoran widow
staring from the window—wave, that is, from my one-fifth-paid-for
car; it was then that the sky was hung
in sulfurous peach, hung in murky scarves or nylon,
slightly but distinctly light;
then that I could not share my gray face,
that I let my mouth go slack and, barefoot,
crossed the wet cement to pee, and then that my blood was horses,
night ones—hooves; my eyelids, for a month—no, more—
itched viciously at night
and below one eye—about the size of a piece of mica
no longer reflecting—then a patch grew red.
It was then that the six Minervas rose like a Beat hallucination—
open-eyed, yet pupil-less, in the way of certain Roman statues,
standing over twelve-foot tall at the base of Carondelet & Coronado;
then that—just to sample some final, remaining irony—the wisteria,
nearly completely dead on one side of my courtyard, exploded
into maybe 80 purple, graceful blooms in the sudden sun, and the
sodden eucalyptus held up twelve new leaves as the faded paper
of its earlier coins began to fall.
And it was then—right then—(as the six, the leather, saddles,
wooden slatted cider press, the old piano found their way to storage;
copper tub to salvage; a few bicycles to trash) then that the
rumpled laundry festered, thrown, unfolded, on the sofa;
then that the dust collected; then that I gave up making—
even trying to make—the bed; then that the dishes gathered

in the sink until they broke; then that there was no further point
in hiding. And it was then, as always at that time of year, that jasmine
laced the chilling air, scumbling even numbness—
even nests of panic, fear.
Its sweetness undermined resolve. Its scent undid the winter.
It was sunny, 47. It was winter, 32.
Padlocks shut the seven doors.
It was all night, then.

K.R. Morrison

MOON SKIN

they say her skin is so thin

> his footprint stays for decades
> memory marks far more vandalizing
> than a lover's little lifetime.

they say her skin is so thin

> she feels everything, so she
> summons sea storms, she
> conjures outbursts, her own
>
> feet graffiti kicks up lover dust
> cauldrons of human tides
> conjured by her inner terrain.

they say her skin is so thin

> she sirens
> our monsters
> we bury
>
> we face
> ourselves
> our maelstroms

when she is full.
When she
is her most sensitive.

Chris Tannahill

21ST CENTURY DEATH POEM

How is it we are tempted to ignore love, wonder at the guillotine
its charm and laugh at it like children?
circling 'round the idea of death as if it were the only thing worth orbiting
did you finally become so tired of the hangman's lime, of Othello's final hold
or was it laziness my dear, did you see it in your mind one day cutting roses?
the cure for French aristocracy – that machine which leaves no angel room to move

Dying is so different from anything we've ever done yet
I'd like to think I've had some practice for I'd lit it all up with the motels and the matches
burned myself down, but my life is the specter that still stands menacingly upright
through every song of exile, driven by some mighty lion of sunlight – up
with each horror after another, slaved into the rarified air of cathedrals and pyramids – up

Believe me, you can't get out of here unless you've a sixth or seventh gear
like James Dean at an intersection
but I am done living inside the light of eyes that go out
of a vision that changes with the blackout and will not yield her real name

As your tears have hooks, there is a galaxy chandelier hanging in my soul that hurts
because this is a willed extinction, a zero-gravity fire in every direction
tracking in the black, divine savagery, Shiva dancing,
a Delphic swerve to the left, a ghost in the road and I cannot turn around

I am what I have lost and at times so buried by the very air once
this darkness becomes
what the living light should kiss
or when my demons wake using the names of saints
and like sleep take us where we cannot

Such a foreign flower of so much power with me in this
slaughterhouse waltz
like an argument won from silence
this is not something you can hold off with a pistol-gripped
crucifix
it is a love that comes down upon us anyway

Don Kingfisher Campbell

IN THE SEA OF DOLPHINS, I AM A MANTA RAY

Dive into the sun to find opened eyes
An empty sky, full of ghosts

Smile because trees become bare
Carcasses on snowy streets

A monkey dreamt the cosmos, found a house
To sit in, gaze at an apple, stare at a fist

Pray in the wilderness, he said
We might as well be ants

But the scientific mind was high on civilization
They celebrated our rocks and roles

Envisioned the perfect you
Driving a lonely night freeway

Galloping to repopulate the stars
And play the game of movement through air

Read a poem on the shore, the sad cliffs watching
Us, eventually eaten by the shark mountain

As the lords in welkin have already seen
Ancient temple women in flames

Our babies litter the world like clouds
Say, hi god, teach me something

Majid Naficy

I WAS BORN BETWEEN TWO WAVES

I was born between two waves
And my life was written on sand.

I was a teenage poet with disheveled hair
Who on the Caspian shore
Hid my sorrows
In the happy breasts of a girl.
One day she disappeared
In her father's gaze.
I threw myself at the sand in rage
And let the wave pull me toward the sea.

Then I returned as a defiant student
And far from the gaze of patrol
Wrote on the sandy surface of an intertidal zone:
"Long live Freedom!
Long last the union of fishermen and rice-growers!"

Now I am an immigrant
Warmed by a half bottle of vodka
Burying the sorrows of seven years in exile
In the shallow waters of the Pacific
And with each empty bottle
Returning to the shore
I let out a cry of joy.

James Cagney

PROPOSAL

I make pilgrimage to the ancient temple of the sea
to construct an altar
of hydrangeas & grape hyacinths
& propose to you, my ocean,
in your evening gown of lilac and fuchsia.

Take the diamond sparks sizzling through my palm.
Let me bring the hurricane
& lay a bouquet of sunken ships
full of watermelon & coconut in your private lagoon.

Let these timid fingers soothe your capillary waves
while you drop stitch centuries of quilted foam.
To you, time & its trivia is a running joke.
Go on -- laugh the sun down
while I wipe the sandpipers from the corners of your eyes.

I have been taking cowrie shells for antidepressants.
God help my superstitious doctors,
prescribing drugs that make society appear to be okay.

Cleanse me down to my pilot light
here at the beginning of all waters
where spirit burns like a bonfire at dawn.

Joseph Millar

ONE DAY

Everything shimmers
with the sound of the train
rattling over the bridge
especially the ears and nostrils and teeth
of the horse riding out
to the pasture of death
where the long train runs
on diesel fuel
that used to run on coal.
I keep listening
for the crickets and birds
and my words fall down below.

I mistook the train for a thunder storm,
I mistook the willow tree
for a home, it's nothing to brag about
when you think of it
spending this time all alone.
I wandered into the hay field
and two tics jumped in my hair
they dug in my scalp
and drank up my blood
 like the sweet wine of Virginia,
then left me under the Druid moon
down here on earth in the kingdom.

Nelson Gary

SHOT

The house emptied of all presences
But mine not grilled by sunbeams
To answer this night, rays held over
In memories with their persistence
Of burn in visions of autumn-leaf
Flames fallen void of ambulance
Shame. The overdose on the past
Has its triggers in the cowardly,
Predatory coyote yowl near trashcans
By curbs filled with dead flowers,
The petals frosted by uneaten birthday
Cake. Older, I don't wait for the voice
To transform my tongue into a whip
That rewinds the tape into a street
Of scars, which scorch the stars.
In this empty house, I don't raise
My voice to the solar past to return
As present blasted from a shotgun.
I have never wanted children; one grin
Slitting the throat of the cosmos is enough.

Richard Modiano

A NEW WORLD IN OUR HEARTS

You can taste it in the shock and roar
of a first, unexpected kiss,
or in the blood in your mouth
that instant after an accident when you realize you're still alive.
It blows in the wind you feel on the rooftops of a really reckless
night of adventure.
You hear it in the magic of your favorite songs,
how they lift and transport you in ways
that no science or psychology could ever account for.
It might be you've seen evidence of it scratched into bathroom walls
in a code without a key,
or you've been able to make out a pale reflection of it
in the movies they make to keep us entertained.
It's in between the words when we speak of our desires and
aspirations,
still lurking somewhere beneath the limitations of being "practical"
and "realistic."
When poets and radicals stay up until sunrise,
wracking their brains for the perfect sequence of words or deeds
to fill hearts (or cities) with fire,
they're trying to find a hidden entrance to it.
When children escape out the window to go wandering late at
night,
or freedom fighters search for a weakness in government
fortifications,
they're trying to sneak into it.
They know better than us where the doors are hidden.
When teenagers vandalize a billboard to provoke all-night chases
with the police,
or anarchists interrupt an orderly demonstration to smash the
windows of a corporate chain store,
they're trying to storm its gates.
When you're making love and you discover a new sensation or
region of your lover's body,
and the two of you feel like explorers discovering a new part of the
world

on a par with a desert oasis or the coast of an unknown continent,
as if you are the first ones to reach the north pole or the moon,
you are charting its frontiers.
It's not a safer place than this one —
on the contrary, it is the sensation of danger there that brings us back to life:
the feeling that for once, for one moment that seems to eclipse the past and future,
there is something real at stake.
Maybe you stumbled into it by accident, once, amazed at what you found.
The old world splintered behind and inside you,
and no physician or metaphysician could put it back together again.
Everything before became trivial, irrelevant, ridiculous as the horizons
suddenly telescoped out around you and undreamt-of new paths offered themselves.
And perhaps you swore that you would never return,
that you would live out the rest of your life electrified by that urgency,
in the thrill of discovery and transformation — but return you did.
Common sense dictates that this world can only be experienced temporarily,
that it is just the shock of transition, and no more;
but the myths we share around our fires tell a different story:
we hear of women and men who stayed there for weeks, years,
who never returned,
who lived and died there as heroes.
We know, because we feel it in that atavistic chamber of our hearts
that holds the memory of freedom from a time before time,
that this secret world is near, waiting for us.
You can see it in the flash in our eyes,
in the abandon of our dances and love affairs,
in the protest or party that gets out of hand.
You're not the only one trying to find it.
We're out here, too… some of us are even waiting there for you.
And you should know that anything you've ever done or considered doing to get there is
not crazy, but beautiful, noble, necessary.
Revolution is simply the idea we could enter that secret world and never return;
or, better, that we could burn away this one, to reveal the one beneath entirely.

Jerry the Priest

SKY THROWING BULLETS OF HAIL

Slathered in Autumn with its sudden sleet flurries and palette of impressionist gauche. Afternoon sky a close-up animated short of God's Red Hand, shooting tourmaline rays into silk hat clouds, whose silver buckles—steady comrades!—unclasp in chameleon fits of nickel/bronze/sterling, now platinum, next molten kaleidoscope bliss.

It's been raining three days straight, if that tells you anything; sky throwin' bullets of hail. Stove's gone out. There's no electricity. I'm writing at a wooden table, by lamplight, to a woman, a Cowsil, a mystery. There's no pattern to this. It just happened that way.

I thought—THINKING—I didn't think at all. I felt or maybe dreamed we had aspects in common. Our delusions. Our take on Babylon.

Listen: I'm a wilderness explorer, hardcore
I adore anthropological extremes
I raid what and where I have to
I don't show up on radar screens

I've been wrong and I've been left. But when you reached across the wire and kissed my ears with laughter I felt blessed, and so did you. Which was unusual, we agreed. And so we stopped, two as one, and went outside and made a wish

...didn't we?

Kim Dower

DOING NOTHING

I lie down on my bed, pretend to read
On the Road, the book I always lie about
having read. I stare out the window
think about the day Miss Josephs,
my fifth grade teacher, shared my book report
on *The Red Pony* with the class:
an example of really excellent work!
But today I'm doing nothing, just staring
at my fingernails. I choose to believe
the latest research, that doing nothing can lead
to bursts of creativity, ideas flowing
like a revitalized creek through a ghost town.
Lava can erupt from an inactive volcano.
I get up from the bed and sit on the floor
in a half spinal twist, apologize to the dead,
which takes a few hours since many people I love
have recently died. *I'm sorry I didn't come over sooner,*
I tell my mother; *sorry, dad, I made fun of you
when you said things like "he's as old as the hills."*
I'm sorry to a poet who loved me.
To be precise, and completely fair to myself,
the word "doing" in front of the word "nothing" changes
the word nothing– lifts it into the world of action.
I realize this as I stare at the electrical outlet,
wonder what I should plug into it,
what kind of lamp might work well in that corner.
Maybe one of those tall skinny metal poles,
three bulbs shooting straight up --
something to illuminate the ceiling, but nah,
it'll look cheap, out of style, and anyway,
maybe I should keep one part of the room dark,
so ideas might grow like mushrooms, populate
my brain with plans I won't pursue.
It might be time to *really* read *On the Road*,
but another's stream of consciousness

competing with my own might incite an inertia tsunami.
I'm sorry to the dogs I loved but never cleaned up after.
I'm sorry for all the time I wasted as a child,
when doing nothing was all they expected of the girl
with the chalkboard and dolls.

Mariano Zaro

AT THE STUDIO

my dance teacher tells
                            me
my dance teacher gives
                            me
a stone

heavy
dense
warm
in my left hand
                            my dance teacher
tells me to hold
                            smooth
                            bigger than a big fist
                            bigger than a big heart
tells me to dance
                            a stone
                            the first step
to dance
                            now
                            and one, two, three, four

and I dance
                            lopsided
                            tilted
                            slanted
                            askew

the first step
I dance
                            embarrassment

my dance teacher tells
                            me

    to dance

                happy embarrassment

                we all carry stones, you know

    my dance teacher tells
                me

                just look around

Linda Noel

THE READING WAS A BENEFIT

Make your checks payable
To Squaw Valley Writers Conference

And like mushrooms break through
Damp but tough earth after rain
    The poem arcs
    The circle in motion
Words fall out of Pacific fog
As the woman behind me repeats
Each word precisely while
Her husband pens the check

    The donation to scholarship
And as his signature dries she asks

Do you know what a squaw is?

    Halting the rocking motion of my feet

I don't know why they keep using that name
It's terrible

My rocking commences as her
Words roll down my back
With the fog

    How poetry raises its head

Where words fall out
Of the mouth of fate

    My thanks are prayers

And I can't cry for
Poetry or for history in
This fog light
Waiting for a poetry reading
    On the Barbary Coast
Because the tears might flood the bay

Stephen Meadows

ON THE ROAD BEFORE RAIN

Over towards Coquille
I watch the rain come
the bruise of it softening
the jagged logged ridge
From this barn roof
Banging down the wide nails
a foot at a time
no one sees cleaner
the quick track of this storm
chasing the blue stone road
up river to the peaks
the farmhouse away near the creek
now swallowed by weather
its chimney smoke scattered
in the moments just before
the first cold waves of mist
bury the barn

Terry Adams

BREATH

They told me when I awoke to this body
      each breath will taste my blood
with the tongue of every creature that has lived,
      and I said yes.
And the air I breathe will be torn by rocks
      abraded by fans and bruised in the factories
of steel, and I said yes.
And they said the ants have a right to this breath
      as much as I, and it erases their paths
as they walk and as easily,
      it erases mine.
They said my breath will read me from inside
      with its licking torch as if I were a cave,
and I said yes.
And the air will carry the breathless
      patience of stone and the seething heat
of asphalt and scatter me from the memories
      as flickeringly as footsteps,
and I said yes,
The air will stir the wet of my body
      in the ocean of bodies, and in shared bodies
of hives and cities, and in the poisons,
      and I said yes,
I will breathe air that has passed through the nail holes
      punched by children into jar lids
to save the lives of fireflies, and I say yes.
      I will breathe the force that blows windrows
in snow, and rubs waves in the sand,
      strips topsoil from farmlands
and makes the cypress cringe from the sea.

Though it is sour with dreams and loud
            with sickness it will run beside my heart
                        like a young girl beside a horse,
it will forgive my legs for running,
            and chase my mind away
from its fear, and I say yes,
            I will blow into whirlwinds in the breath
of my lover, and into sea storms I will fly to be healed,
            and to the vastness inside clouds I will go
for rest, and I will wash out my tears
            with the mist blown from white caps,
and disperse my venom in daggers of sunlight,
            and I say yes,
I will torture my vision through
            with the everlasting scanning of seabirds, yes,
            I will breathe each layer from the horizon,
and hush my thoughts in the deepest calm of caves,
            and ripple the slow, sunken rivers, like sleep,
then whistle through blow-holes hidden in thickets
            linking the underground to the sky.
I will whisper through the perforated coinage of sewer lids,
            I will lie down in hot valleys with the breath
of vegetables, and I will say yes.
I will breathe a clear cloud of silk around my heart,
            and wear a frayed scarf of fire,
I will breathe what determines the path
            of falling feathers,
and blows the snow from the seared summits
            of mountains. I will stay trapped
a thousand years in a tomb until a mouse will free me.
            I will blow a cloud on the final mirror
of the dying, before the cistern of silence cracks,
and I will make a quick slate
            for fingers shouting behind cold glass,
saying yes.

Harold Norse

NORTH BEACH
For Alix Geluardi

in the Coffee Gallery Bob Kaufman sings *Summertime*
shakes my hand asking What do you see when you look at George
    Washington?
I say The American Revolution the big breasts of a hermaphrodite
The White Man is God laughs Bob as he dances drunk
clutching a battered anthology of lonely North Beach poetry
raw from the burning ghats of bars and human wrecks
Salvaged from speed and junk and booze and
one-night stands

the tape deck plays soap opera music to our tragic script
out of it we make poetry
like sudden life
like the shock of light

the drunken sound from a motley crew
Linda Lovely down Grant Avenue
Eileen in shawls and dresses of colored threads
threads of the beat beauty of peyote
in the flow of pills and weed in Blabbermouth night
I have seen 20 barechested drummers
getting stoned on rooftops says Eileen
chronicler of obsessive visions
Would you wear my eyes? asks Bob

they broke down each other's doors
hocked typewriters and record players
lied, screamed, jumped from windows
died and fell in love
those poets and painters you hung on Marina walls
and visited in prison
in parks waterfronts bars cheap hotels
an ocean of missing persons
departed poets leaving no address

orchestrating distances
in temporary shelters

San Francisco, 1973

Tongo Eisen-Martin

A SKETCH ABOUT GENOCIDE

A San Francisco police chief says, "Yes, you poets make points. But they are all silly,"

Police chief sowing a mouth onto a mouth
Police chief looking straight through the poet

Flesh market both sides of the levy
Change of plans both sides of the nonviolence

              On no earth
              Just an earth character

His subordinate says, "Awkward basketball moves look good on you, sir... Yes, we are everywhere, sir... yes, unfortunately for now, white people only have Black History ... we will slide the wallpaper right into their cereal bowls, sir ... Surveil the shuffle."

I am a beggar and all of this day is too easy
I want to see all of the phases of a wall
Every age it goes through
              Its humanity
            Its environmental racism

We call this the ordeal blues
Now crawl to the piano seat and make a blanket for your cell
Paint scenes of a child dancing up to the court appearance
And leaving a man,
        but not for home

Atlantic ocean charts mixed in with parole papers
Mainstream funding (the ruling class's only pacifism)

Ruling class printing judges (fiat kangaroos)
Making judges hand over fist
Rapture cop packs and opposition whites all above a thorny stem
Caste plans picked out like vans for the murder show
anglo-saints addicting you to a power structure

you want me to raise a little slave, don't you?
bash his little brain in
and send him to your civil rights

No pain
Just a white pain

Delicate bullets in a box next to a stack of monolith scriptures
       (makes these bullets look relevant, don't it?)

                                      I remember you
              Everywhere you lay your hat is the capital of the south
                        The posture you introduced to that fence
                      The fence you introduced to political theory

                                  If you shred my dreams, son
                                  I will tack you to gun smoke

                            The suburbs are finally offended

                              this will be a meditation too

Eric Morago

SMOLDER

On my way to work, there is a fire
burning along the highway,
flames dancing like a stripper
on a pole made of jet fuel.

Everyone pulls over to the shoulder;
they get out of their cars to watch,
to take pictures.

#morningcommute
#destruction
#holyshit

The blaze draws their wonder,

as though Prometheus himself
came down, rubbed the two
sticks together, as if

they never saw a thing burn before.

But I used to scorch—

used to feel my heart swell
so red I thought a devil
lived in my chest, spiking
my poetry like punch at prom.

I'd combust into such protest
people used to stop, gather
and share their stories of ghosts
around my glow, and I'd burn
to bring light to their dark.

That was before a mortgage.

Now I make a manager's salary,
not a writer's singe—suffer
a commute five days a week,
and find glaciers forming under
ribs that once framed a furnace.

Budgets are due and I spend
more time writing emails
than I do poems.

Later the news reports on the fire—
how it was started by a homeless man
trying to cook his dinner.

I hear this and I envy him, his hunger,
his need to survive—to spark
flint to feast, despite risk

of smolder and ash.

He knows full well his gamble—
how it could consume,
how even if swallowed up
by that very desire to live,

at least he would go belly full,
torch to his own funeral pyre,
with a parade of onlookers

to see him off, their phones
stretched towards the sky,
cameras flashing brilliant.

#tribute

David L. Ulin

OUR SON COMES OVER

it's the second week of
August and already I have
spent too much time with too many
people, inhaled their breath,
their flumes from the other side
of an outdoor table or within
an enclosed living room
what do vaccines mean
in the face of Delta
or Lambda or Omega
which will be
the variant that kills us all
what I mean is
there are crossroads in our future
although (of course) that is how it always is
and yet I don't want to dwell
on that this evening, better to inhabit
the moment while it lingers
before we have to hide
ourselves away again
our boy stopping by
on his drive from work
for takeout dinner
my wife and I so thrilled to
visit with him you might think
we had discovered
a brand new source of joy
yes, there are crossroads in our future
trouble riding at our left shoulder
like a car coming up fast in the sideview
on a highway late at night
when you are somewhere
you have not been before
and the pavement is an empty river
and you feel lost

not knowing where to turn
which is the direction home
in a life where we are stalked by death
we are ever having to decide
so we sit at the table
with our son, our beloved
who has come over to see us
aware of the risk but also recognizing
that risk is (how could it be otherwise)
the only way of love

Amélie Frank

CHALCEDONY

Would it surprise you to know
that the heart is not red in its truest sense?
It is actually a green place
more of a malachite
not so flashy as emerald
not so humble as moss.
The good ones are neither proud nor base
and they are never truly as hard
as you believe they can become
as you believe your own has become
as my own can never become
despite its misadventures and narrow escapes.

I think I understand the heart better
than you might, because I don't think
it makes us fools. I think it makes us genuine
and shame on those who fear or abuse
the secret color of its nature.
Certainly, passion is notorious for running red
but the nourishing, protective aspect
of the heart is the truest and lushest green imaginable.
What gives shade? What is a tonic to the blood?
What kind of thinking will save the planet?
What will unroll at our feet should we ever manage
to get outdoors?

What color are my eyes?
What color are my eyes when I look at you?

Christine No

PRAYER FOR THE SEASON

I am a woman, abated, a city-block upturned.
Four-alarm fire, tongue held in a cage match,
I am a phone-call refused, an exceptional façade

> *It takes a village to raise a monster*

I am a whole village razed.

> *Oh, Executioner,*
> *Show me how she got inside*
> *Show me where the fire started*
> *Show me where I lost my wallet*

Where rot began, where fester
Left a bloodbath:

Whole auditoriums spellbound
Gasoline in the drain, heads severed all
Ventriloquists dragged & quartered
Tongue-evicted

Mumbled a tone-deaf Hosanna
Dumbfounded—*Lord, save us!*

> *This world is open season*

Whole intersections stopped
at massacre & crosshair. The
corners unaccounted—

Bless Our Valiant Failures, Late Bloomers
to the Schoolyard, The Sitting Duck, alone

> *This world is open wound*

Lord, Bless The Prodigal Arson
The Self-appointed Executioner,
The Vengeful, Sullen Queen
They come hunting—

Glory, their inheritance!
Pockets full of teeth & evidence

& Lord, Bless the rest of us
The Blissful Useless

    This world is open season

Easy Targets, split wide

    — open wound

& Won't you keep us
Helpless Onlookers?

Our best intentions
Our wrung hands,
Our rubbernecks?

Frank X. Gaspar

CAN'T YOU HEAR THE WIND HOWL?

I'm shivering here with Coleman Hawkins and a cup of gin
and no idea what hour of the night it is—feeling ashamed
of how time passes when everyone knows I should be
the responsible party and put a stop to all this waste. What good
is a night if there's always a dawn lurking somewhere in the future?
How can I be completely certain of the stars if they fade
so easily before such cheap theatrics? When will I learn, as all
my betters have, to live in the moment? Out in the alley there's
a possum looking for a home. Out in the city lights there's an
alley looking for a street. You can hear the wind blowing
all along the window screens. It's singing to the voices in my head,
it's saying, *quiet!* It's saying, *Shooo!* Coleman Hawkins isn't
saying a word. He's occupied with some friends. He's living
in the moment with certain characters with names like Dizzy
and Django and Pee Wee and Cozy. He ain't going nowhere,
he is all past and future, if you know what I mean. I don't have
the nerve to say my heart is aching—not with *that* crew all
around me, not with that bass line shaking the books in their
cracked spines and rocking the pens and pencils. Am I wrong?
Am I wrong to let Cicero rest awhile and let Sappho, in her
tatters, sleep under the seven sisters, and to breathe in deeply
and to breathe out deeply? And to let the ice in my blue cup bark
in its quiet cataclysms and let the brown air blow down a hundred
miles
from the deserts because I have no choice in these matters? Now
let me tap my foot in a certain way. In a certain way because there
was a machine once that could cull every kind of music from a room
and save it for a while, unharmed. Can't you hear the wind howl?
Here all around my feeble senses? Here in the iron lung of the
night?
Here it comes again, all teeth in the palm leaves, looking for a home.

Kevin Opstedal

THE SMOG'S VIBRANT GOWN

Beauty or not a recompense
my compass
          "a paper moon above a cardboard sea"
& so forth
        in a homemade hazmat suit

odds & evens (love assumes) shadow games

as if to tip a hand
already played

          the same turning back the same
                parting of the reeds

& the fog unfurls
inspiring dewy-eyed parking lot rhapsodies
held together w/duct tape & rhyme
lifted like a chalice rag
to be folded neatly & tucked away in a
dark green corner of the surf

lowering the boom

somewhere in the region of Petey Wheatstraw
or Emily Dickinson

        but w/heavy waves rocking the pier the
swagger & stoke of it
            w/the passing of parochial time
& the countdown 10, 9, 8, 7-come-11 . . .

Ask for what you want
blink & it's gone
who knows where it comes from desire

Greer Nakadegawa-Lee

SEPTEMBER 24TH, WAITING AT THE BART STATION AHEAD OF YET ANOTHER CLIMATE STRIKE

There is something stuck in my heart or in my throat
from which there are no exits.

Today everything is crashing down,
though the people on the street don't know it,

we are all aware of liars stalking through places of power,
thrusting elbows and knees and pecking at the mesh of our coops,
we're all aware of the squabbling squawking bodies, yes.

There is nothing quite like the reminder passed down through
generations that we will never be the people our ancestors were,
that our grandchildren will live suffocated or bombed out and it's
because we take our cars on the road and drive to the beach,
because we plug our phones in at night and go back to school
shopping and apply for jobs at CVS,

can you hear yourself over the infernal destitution
of brokenhearted adults?
All looking at you with pity and anger and running their
fingers over stranger's tattoos,
God, I just wanted my own turn at ruining the world but
I have to pretend to be its mad savior,

That's a confession when we kiss and hold our own hearts
to our chest,
selfish love,
unconsumable and unmonetizable,

Some of us did want to live in our own corner of the world
but then we had to grow up.

Larry Colker

CROSSING OVER (EXHIBIT #204)

Somehow I have arrived in a strange land.
It turns out I speak the language
and there are people I seem to know.

Here I find the Larry Colker Museum,
disturbingly close to completion—
locked in glass cases
the blue wooden top my father taught me to spin,
the bare arm and shoulder of a young girl,
the first kiss,
the varsity letters,
the razor blade,
the recurrent dream of flying and falling,
the letters full of half-truths and cowardice....

There is not enough heat in this place,
and I can't get used to everything turning gray—
buildings, food, flowers, hands, eyes.
Music gets harder to hear.

At the other end of the hall is a small child crying,
asking his parents if they can go home now.

Ann Menebroker

ALLEY-HOUSE THINKING

What I really want to do
is put my mouth over yours
stick my tongue
into your thoughts
stir up
more than Heidegger's
last wet dream.
Why don't you like
long, wet kisses
anyway?
What I want to do
is water the geraniums
outside, then
come back in
and lie down
naked beside you, the
big song of the bed
drawing us
into its watery refuge
letting the bodies
do the work
of what love says best.
I take back one thing:
let's make love first,
and then
bother the flowers
from their dry living.

Sylvia Ross

MATRILINEAGE

The only picture I have
Of my great-grandmother
Shows her lying
In her coffin.
No one thought to take
A picture of the Chukchansi
Woman
Until time had passed away.

The best picture I have
Of my grandmother
Shows here holding
Her sister's stillborn boy
He was a fat and beautiful baby.
She looks down at him.
Seems like no one
In my family
Thinks about time
Until it's gone.

I have lots and lots
Of pictures of my mother, but
None show her
Standing in a kitchen,

Apron stretched
Across her fat belly,
Dimples winking
From her round cheeks
As she tells some truth
Funnier than lies.

Michelle Bitting

AN EXERCISE IN LOVE
~ *after Diane di Prima*

I was remembering with Gail
over coffee in Topanga how I
used to choke up thinking
about my son's transition—about
  the dresses of many colors
  no longer needed we'd
  slipped like pretty fish
  from their wires
  inside his closet's unlit shell
and floated to a thrifty coastal
store. I suppose there are moments
together, inhaling a favorite
indie film or albacore rolls
  at an L.A. eatery when
  I've caught the eyes
  of strangers squinting at him
  from behind their pebbly
centerpieces, like stunned sea
anemones when the sun
pokes an altar of clouds
and muscles them open, blessing
a son's sacred face that is pure
  moonstones and cherubs
  and green hills and herons
  at dawn, little sea grass
  tufts woven on the wind
  of his chin's pocked shore
due to regular hormone injections. I
suddenly understand how confused we
all are, how utterly wrong we've
gotten it thus far, us dinosaurs, us old

      barges, backwards in our dreams
      of absolute gender and pleasure,
      until Gail and I are nodding again
      across the distance of a canyon
      table as I lift a toasted slice, seeded
with pomegranate, sigh a cool scarf
of breeze into my cup's hot shade.
She understands. My son who I love
is just Emmet. *Just Emmet*, my mouth is saying
      over, and like no other—Emmet—
      entirely himself, his name, his own.

Charlie Getter

"THE LAST <<TRUE>> YUGOSLAV"

Silence suits us in these times
because no one believes what we
believe anymore

One time we held the banner for
        a great idea

but it doesn't exist anymore

maybe it never did

or maybe the tripe that we're fed
of ideas being more powerful
                than anything
                was itself
      just a bad idea

I don't miss my Christianity
but no matter what you could say
about it
      it at least paid lip service
      to there being divinity
      in everybody

and though no one acted
      accordingly

it was an inescapable notion

      no longer

      now it's just tribes
      shaken into a
      zero sum

I won
 you lose
 and consequently
 we all lose

but I stand proud
grinning in my delusion

    as the last true yugoslav

    thinking prejudice is bad
    no matter where it comes from

    and it's only bad people
        who judge
        other people

    by their genetic affiliations

as the world keeps finding
    new ways to burn

    inside hearts
        inside minds

because when prejudice
is cloaked as justice

there can be no peace

and if this is how it is going to be
    there will never be peace
if there ever was

    except here, under my coat
        under my skin

    which I hope I
        thick enough

    to protect
        yugoslavia

Jack Brewer

THIS IS WILMINGTON

Retune my guitar
Till it plays my Father's chords
And takes me back to Harbor Park
Where I can sleep ole Hollywood off
In my C – street dreams
My Metro starts
And sprints Avalon

Where Jack still waits
Paul keeps faith
The 232 is late
There are no parades

But the Don Hotel stands higher
Than the Catalyst Cracking Tower
And that gives everyone hope in Wilmington
That gives everyone a home in Wilmington

Where the heart beats in harbor
Figueroa was born
To the first son Banning
Who gave up the land deeds
For the Mothers in canneries,
The father's refineries
Where the sailors pawn their sextants
Till the next ship comes in
And it always does
Because everything, everyone returns to Wilmas

Don't go to the north side
To hustle bottles
Unless you know Dago
And don't deliver your papers there
Cause they'll never pay you there
Anyway, the dogs run free

The bad kids are tied to porches
But no one gets hurt
Who's not where they don't belong
And the east-siders
And the west-siders wear this
And face off on Avalon

Where Jack still waits
Paul Uriaz keeps faith
The 232 is late
There are no parades

Seko Bro's remain
The Mahar boys still sing oldies
Tony Blass spars in the shadows
Till the street lights go out
Then comes Sunday morning
Little children walk themselves
To Saint Peter and Paul's
As the Vejos look into the din
Of the Wilmington cemetery

Tate Swindell

BRANDED

Today
at lunch
with Pierre
We spoke of horror stories
from election day
The continual thread
around the warehouse
early mornings
when breath
is better seen
than heard

Tho
more
comical
than
painful

And this fits
since politics
is such a joke
                in America
                                    these days

Basing on money

As people fail
to acknowledge
that we vote
with our dollars
tho some
with only cents
leftover change
from dues paid
on three-fifths

America is not a country

America is a marketing concept

S.F.
9/16/21

Joan Jobe Smith Voss

"BUK RHYMES WITH PUKE," CHARLES BUKOWSKI SAID TO THE LADY AT THE LIQUOR STORE IN THE 1973 TAYLOR HACKFORD DOCUMENTARY *BUKOWSKI*

Bukowski wanted to go with me and Anais Nin in 1975
to meet Henry Miller still alive up there in Pacific Palisades.
"Miller's my favorite writer!" Bukowski exclaimed, often
emulating Miller, some critics said, but what did I know, I hadn't yet
read much of Henry Miller and Bukowski would write so many
books the next 10 years, how could I ever keep track?

Anais Nin had never read this Charles Bukowski L.A.
Poet Man I wanted to bring with me to go meet Henry Miller,
nor had she seen the Taylor Hackford PBS
documentary "Bukowski"
and I was a nervous wreck about the whole thing, driving with
Buk that rhymed with puke, Buk chug-a-lugging beer/vodka/gin
et al on the way to Anais Nin's house on Hildago Drive in L.A.
And: where would they sit in my little bitty VW Bug? Anais
in the front
seat scrunched beside me? Buk in the back seat all boozy woozy?

Henry Miller hardly ever drank booze; he had a bad stomach, age
80something and not into partying and WHAT would Anais Nin
think
of this unpredictable, love dog from Hell poet man Buk that
rhymed with puke
who'd maybe break one of Miller's windows like he had
Ferlinghetti's,
pretend to urinate in a champagne bottle and then pretend
to drink it like
he had at the party I gave in his honor. For sure he'd grab her
and French kiss her.

Would she like it? Scream? Push Buk off a palisade?
Or maybe Bukowski'd
capture her heart in his hands and she'd fall in love at first
sight with Buk,
she age 72, Bukowski a young stud boy toy at the time,
only age 55 in 1975.

Maybe Buk would've fallen in love with her, too, write a book
of poems
about Anais's still-graceful dancer's body, her big, beautiful eyes,
sexy-sweet
smile and push ME off a palisade, the 2 of them alone amongst
the L.A.
palms and manzanita and yuccas to do a 2-some tango atop
the double-"O's"
of the Hollywood sign. But I'll never know. Because my
terry-poo doggie
named Daisy got sick and I spent all day at the
veterinarian's wondering
WHAT
might've happened that day
had things been different.

Soheyl Dahi

LUNCHES WITH LINDA

Sure, we talked about Bukowski
but not every time
Those lunches with Linda
watching her eat and
talk in that marvelous accent
about being a woman
a Mormon
a patient in an insane asylum
a wife, a mother, a lover
an artist, poet, sculptor
and struggling for the fucking dollar
like the rest of us

Some days
she was not well
she held my arm
as we crossed the street
to our favorite Chinese restaurant, *8 Immortals*
We drank our beers
and admired the harsh beauty
of a whole Flounder fish, fried
with greens on the side

Only once she broke down
when we were at the Green Apple Books
in the poetry section
I showed her a poem of Bukowski he had written for her
she took the book from me and sank on a chair
reading with tears in her eyes
right there and then
in that silence
I learned all I needed to know
about what went on between her
and Bukowski.

Neeli Cherkovski

FOR UKRAINE

simple enough
not to say anything
let it slide
and watch almond trees
swaying in afternoon wind
of our schoolyard

all the time I thought
of the war in which there will be
no victory, only silence,
only a spare tire left roadside,
one last man
singing "Waltzing Matilda"
on a beach in Australia,
I'd seen it in a movie
when I was a kid

Then we had many wars
around the world
as I sat at lakeside
or hiked into the wilderness,
I'd sit in college classrooms
wanting to say something,
nothing to be said, man is
a fallen leaf, Russian troops
advance through the fields
punishing the world
and making of peace a tattered veil

I should have said something
but I loved the view
from the bluff at Fort Funston
cawing of seabirds
Like airplanes over scrub oak

I wanted to say something
when I was a kid
studying for bar mitzvah,
but the rabbi commanded:
"suffer in silence,
let the nightmare
remain"

now Russian missiles
soar into breadlines
and over heads
of refugees, I'll keep silence
to myself, walk the hall
of our synagogue, 1957,
12 years after Hiroshima

Is there wheat in the fields
even yet? Let us blossom
like roses, may we be
so young

I see Russian troops
making their move, I watch
as people flee
burning embers

I should have been alive
before, that has never been possible,
men tried but failed

Desire huddles in branches of trees,
I stared out
of the classroom window
at the Atomic Age
listening to talks
of nuclear deterrence
I knew we were going to
punish ourselves

if I had spoken
there would be no bread lines,
if I had stood my ground
Ukrainian earth
would rise with the sun

my grandfathers and grandmothers
would have spoken
of the land and its bounty

"Mein father owned a mill,"
Granny said, "near Kyev"
she died and the world died
birds wore cloth
woven of wheat
that was the end
until all spun out of control

This is how I see it
thousands of years
into the future,
bare bones, rapid fire distortions,
out and out lies, China Russia America
Prague Budapest Beijing Rio

do you make a paper crane
out of madness
and lay it before the shrine?

Lawrence Ferlinghetti

SALUTE!

To every animal who eats or shoots his own kind
And every hunter with rifles mounted in pickup trucks
And every private marksman or minuteman with telescopic sight
And every smalltime con or bigtime gangster with gat
And every armed guard and every armed robber
And every redneck in boots with dogs and sawed-off shotguns
And every peace officer with dogs trained to track and kill
And every blackbelt master of any police karate academy teaching
  painless death
And every plainclothesman or private-eye and under-cover agent
  with shoulder-holster full of death
And every servant of the people gunning down people or
  shooting-to-kill fleeing felons
And every Guardia Civile in any country guarding civilians with
  handcuffs and carbines
And every border guard at no matter what Check Point Charley
  on no matter which side of which border Berlin Wall Bamboo or
  Tortilla Curtain
And every elite state trooper highway patrolman in custom-tailored
  riding pants and plastic crash-helmet and shoestring necktie and
  six-shooter in silver-studded holster
And every prowl-car with riot-guns and sirens and every riot-tank
  with mace and tear-gas
And every crack pilot with rockets and napalm under wing and
  every sky-pilot blessing bombers at take-off
And any State Department of any super-state selling guns to
  both sides
And every revolutionary on any side whose gun comes first & last
  in the redemption of mankind
And every nationalist of no matter what nation in no matter what
  world Black Brown or White who kills for his nation

And every prophet or poet with gun or shiv and any enforcer of
   spiritual enlightenment with force and any enforcer of the power
   of any state with Power
And to any and all who kill & kill & kill for Peace
I raise my middle finger
In the only proper salute

Santa Rita Prison, January, 1968

Ellyn Maybe

2016: THE YEAR THE 20TH CENTURY FINALLY DIED

The year so many musicians died and the year
Freedom seemed to be moving underground
Caskets filled the air.
We live in times of turmoil, clocks beating quicker and quicker.
Middle age seems old.
Seniors seem timeless.

There's a lethargy in the way people move.
There's a liturgy on the tip of our tongues.
There's something in the morning cereal.
It looks like newsprint.
There's something in the evening news.
It seems like farce.

As though this couldn't be real.
This over-the-top peek into tragedy's eyelid.
This shiver that lives in our psyche like snow.
We ski into another winter.
The world is on a ski lift.
Cocoa is leaving its face around a cup.
We stir and it's January.
We stir and it's the 20th Century.
We stir and it looks like it's black and white newsreels.
History tries to repeat itself as the people in power like sequels.
People wear the hero mask, the death mask, the face, and the heart.
People make choices. The stores sell everything.

One of the strongest songs from Rodgers and Hammerstein,
You've Got to Be Carefully Taught,
Prejudging is the name of the game so many households play.
Play rummi kub instead.
Play solitaire, don't be influenced by peers.
One minute to midnight but people don't know if the year
 will leave us dangling from some threshold.
History said, look at me with your eyes aflame.
Burn my pain in your memory.
Walk into the libraries and kiss all the spines.

The Earth is spinning whether people stay on it or not.
What if Earth falls in the forest and nobody is there to hear it.
The last person on Earth will carry a pencil.
That is why Earth has survived this long.

Doug Knott

APOLOGY TO GRETA THUNBERG

You're right about that global warming, kid!
We spent it, we drove it,
we burned it, we fueled it
we rode it, but we didn't pay for it –
Didn't think it was your future, too -

We are your distinguished elders
And came of age just before the peak of the wave,
and we've surfed it to the shore, rolling in like pearls.
We're the coolest, didn't even work for it,
it just got laid on us by the big living earth Gaia -
"Yes" - she said, "take my breast"
and we took her blood, skin and bones, too.

And our generation has enjoyed every possibility of living
whatever we want, wherever we choose to go.
We are the party of freedom - meaning
we partied with freedom

Now we're those hard-boiled eggs in the sunset.
What do you want from us?
Please deliver your rage to our chattering class,
We are the tribe - the human tribe –
And we welcome you to this fat-ball planet
Where we're all born out of God's Word

And when we get hungry
We go out on the crinkle-bulgy landscape
and kill kill a big elephant to feed our tribe.
Lots of meat meat we eat eat
Then dance pray fuck – then pray fuck dance
Afterwards, sleepity-sleep.

Then get up, have coffee -- and make civilization! –
hammocks, clay pots, sexy figurines of gods,
Broadway plays - we create a world of light and dark
Sex, poetry, ocean-going plastic, capitalism, terrorism, religion
A house fantastic for us alone!

Enough – We hungry again!
Let's get another elephant --
Or at least an In-and-Out Burger
There's always more food, isn't there?

It will all work out ...(somehow)
There will be a solution ...(somehow)
But (somehow), all that gets fuzzy when I try to think about it.
I can't shoot that hoop of what to do

You say the only way is massive political action?
No oil, and eat nothing in plastic?
Not a chance, even if everyone else does it!
Who helps who control who?

The earth is so stressed digesting us
Where can it shit, except on you?
So sorry, we knew, but didn't know
and now you know, but what to do?

Also there is no individual guilt,
We're all absolved and complicit.
All I ever did was drive my car and turn on
the house-lights and some air-con --
Me such a tiny, ordinary consumer!

In case the planet might shrug us off
You might consider the intrinsic death-wish of the species.
And all that plastic in the guts of whales?
We share the gifts.

Climate change is a spiritual vaccination
For those of us on the edge of the afterlife.
The seas will rise, the continents fall

I thought I'd never live to see it happen,
But I was wrong.

Richard Brautigan

LET'S VOYAGE INTO THE NEW AMERICAN HOUSE

There are doors
that want to be free
from their hinges to
fly with perfect clouds.

There are windows
that want to be
released from their
frames to run with
the deer through
back country meadows.

There are walls
that want to prowl
with the mountains
through the early
morning dusk.

There are floors
that want to digest
their furniture into
flowers and trees.

There are roofs
that want to travel
gracefully with
the stars through
circles of darkness.

David Meltzer

RE: 2016

Rejoice that we are here
that we love each other
that we treasure & value
each other

Relax in the flux of moments
flowing w/grace

Reveal our core heart
our moment, our possibilities

Revel in the wonders surrounding us

Realize everything & nothing as one

Recognize every second of our impermanence

Retreat into no-self aware

Resist resistance, accept acceptance

Renew our love, our life

Recognize our precious gift
in every moment

Reflection on water changing,
never the same

New Year's Eve
31:Dec:15

francEyE

CALL

I rest as the day warms, hear
through closed windows the faint repeated call
of the fog horn, three miles away. It warns off
sailors but I don't know who those sailors are,
and it warns me: You are not in charge. Your
children can be taken from you,
your life ended over and over
before it is over. Listen,
it says: A voice. That's
all you have.

AFTERWORD
BEAT. NOT BEAT.

Beat. Means something different to everyone on the path. For me it is all things folded into the multi-layered origami of the poetic. Or as the Venice Beats might define it, a creative life in service to The Lady, the muse, process. Applied deliberation and empathy in practice. Beginning to end, whatever it is, it is all, practice and process. All part of the grand dynamic of the enduring poetic.

The mid 20th century phenomenon that came to be known as the Beat Generation birthed in the postwar hustle of Times Square and the academic status quo of Columbia University is too often taken out of context, viewed unfairly thru the prism of the present, deeming the entire period and its impact irrelevant. The Beats were an awakening, a search for alternatives to the cultural and political standards of the day. Creative empaths, seekers moving in new directions. Jews, Catholics, Buddhists, atheists, existentialists, gays, women and people of color were coming together to tell their stories in poetry, art, music, dance and film. A new beginning in a new postwar world being felt and heard in strange new ways that were without question making noise in the conventional void, Beat culture and members of the tribe feared and reviled as norms of the day were being challenged and often shattered.

What began with Walt Whitman and bohemian New York in the late 19th century, moved forward by the ex-patriots of the Lost Generation in France and Europe, and then hit the road with the Beat Generation after the Bomb dropped to usher in the Atomic Age continues to flourish to this day. There are easily thousands across the globe inspired by the musings of the tribe, past and present, who follow and are part of the culture. Many of the surviving first wave, second wave and Baby Beats would tell you that this isn't true, that they are the one and only original issue, no one else need apply. Much the same way that many of the surviving old school punks would tell you that Punk ended before it began, and that all those kids in their ripped Misfit T-shirts, spikes and leather drag are all poseurs. A Baby Boomer cutting my teeth on the 1970s, I don't see or experience what might be Punk as being too far removed from what might be Beat. *They just are.*

I remain guided by spirits, touched by these Beat progenitors, converts and followers every day. Generally, I defer to others. If someone thinks that I am Beat, then maybe I am that mad bird flying backwards. For me, it shall always be my goal to remain in process, where all things are possible. Where the creative reactor benevolently burns for those with a need to *go*. To live openly and creatively without apology.

There are a few that I need to thank personally, individuals who really had my back on this journey. These fellow travelers are the real deal, each one a master class in Beat arts and letters: Soheyl Dahi, Michael C Ford, Brian Hassett, Richard Modiano and Tate Swindell. They honor me with their friendship, craft and knowledge every day. Thanks to fellow editors Alexis Rhone Fancher and Kim Shuck for their hard work and contributions. To Eric Morago, our intrepid publisher, what a beautiful babe. I would also like to give a special shout out to Rich Ferguson, our lead editor, the book's progenitor and my friend. What a true pleasure and honor it has been working you with on this anthology. Thanks for allowing me to be on the road with you.

Not everything or everyone included in this book is Beat, or pretends to be. It was my understanding that Beat was at the center with an extreme focus on California poets, but not necessarily the entire dance for this magnificent anthology. This book has been curated in such a way that it is Beat in origin and association moving in all directions at once to achieve a greater dynamic. I came late to the game, doing what I could to bring forward as many varied voices as was allowed, and in the end, there are still so many worthy voices missing from the final mix.

Keep singing. *Beat is your heart's forwarding address.*

Go!

S.A. Griffin
Los Angeles, CA
June 30, 2022

ABOUT THE AUTHORS

Steve Abee is a teacher and writer, author of *The Bus: Cosmic Ejaculations of the Daily Mind in Transit* and the poetry collection *Great Balls of Flowers* amongst others. He believes that backyards are secret holy sites in all our lives and is grateful for the daily cup of coffee at sunrise.

Terry Adams MC'd an Autumn poetry festival at the SF Beat Museum for 10 years. He rescued and inhabits Ken Kesey's famous 1960's cabin in La Honda and has poems in *Witness, The Sun, Portside, Ironwood, Catamaran, The Painted Bride Quarterly, Poetry,* and elsewhere. He MCs, with Joe Cottonwood, the monthly "Lit Night" in La Honda. His collection, "Adam's Ribs," is available from Off The Grid Press.

Kim Addonizio is the author of a dozen books of poetry and prose. Her most recent poetry collection is *Now We're Getting Somewhere* (W.W. Norton). Her memoir-in-essays, *Bukowski in a Sundress*, was published by Penguin. She has received NEA and Guggenheim Fellowships, Pushcart Prizes in both poetry and the essay, and her poetry has been widely translated and anthologized. *Tell Me* was a National Book Award Finalist in poetry. She lives in Oakland, CA. www.kimaddonizio.com

Linda J. Albertano (1942-2022) has unleashed her vocabulary at the John Anson Ford Theater, Lollapalooza and SXSW. She was among those representing Los Angeles at the One World Poetry Fest in Amsterdam. For the LA Theatre Center, she unveiled "Joan of Compton…" complete with poets, dancers and a 30-piece marching band from South Central LA. Albertano also presented at Allen Ginsberg's Memorial at the Wadsworth Theater. And she's featured on the Venice Poetry Monument with Wanda Coleman and Charles Bukowski.

Will Alexander - His work beginning to lean in the direction of 50 published works. He not only is a poet, novelist, playwright, aphorist, philosopher, visual artist, pianistic improvisor. Poet-in-residence Beyond Baroque. He lives in Los Angeles.

RD Armstrong aka **Raindog** has been a poet for over 50 years. Recently, he retired because of health issues. He doesn't miss the hoopla! Now he donates money to the poetry world. Says it's *"More rewarding!"*

Danny Baker (1969-2020) was raised in Los Angeles, landing him as an outcast in the center of the '80s punk rock scene as a wild teen in the streets. He would move to New York and transform himself into a successful mover and shaker on Wall Street. Danny's first book of poems, *Fractured*, was the debut release on Punk Hostage Press (2012). Other books included *Death in the Key of Life* (Oneiros Books. 2014).

Ellen Bass's most recent book is *Indigo* (Copper Canyon Press, 2020). She coedited the first major anthology of women's poetry, *No More Masks!* (Doubleday, 1973) and cowrote the groundbreaking *The Courage to Heal* (Harper Collins, 1988, 2008). Her awards include Fellowships from the Guggenheim Foundation, the California Arts Council, and The Lambda Literary Award. Her poems frequently appear in *The New Yorker* and many other magazines. A Chancellor of the Academy of American Poets, Bass founded poetry workshops at various prisons and teaches at Pacific University.

Judith Ayn Bernhard is a founding member and past chair of Marin Poetry Center. She is the author of a book of poems, *Prisoners of Culture*. Her most recent work is *Marriages*, a collection of short prose pieces. She lives with her husband, Byron Spooner, in San Francisco.

Iris Berry is an author, L.A. historian, actress, and musician. In the 1980s & 90s, she wrote, performed, and recorded with bands such as the Lame Flames, the Ringling Sisters, and the Dickies. She has served on the Board of Directors for Beyond Baroque Literary/Arts and has received a Certificate of Merit Award from the city of L.A. for her contribution as a writer, and for her charity work. Berry is the co-founder of Punk Hostage Press, where continues to champion and advocate for original voices.

Michelle Bitting was short-listed for the 2020 Montreal International Poetry Prize and named a finalist for the 2021 Coniston Prize and 2020 *Reed Magazine* Edwin Markham Prize. A fourth collection of poetry, *Broken Kingdom* won the 2018 *Catamaran* Prize and was named to *Kirkus Reviews'* Best of 2018. In 2021, her manuscript *Nightmares & Miracles* won the Wilder Prize and will be published by *Two Sylvias Press* in 2022. Michelle is a Lecturer in Poetry and Creative Writing at Loyola Marymount University and Film Studies at U of Arizona Global.

Nikki Blak is a writer, sociologist, womanist, and intersectional feminist whose art interrogates social constructs and affirms Blackness. Her thought leadership and radical education work centers marginalized and oppressed populations in the United States. Born and raised in Los Angeles, Nikki resides on unceded Tongva land with her partner and children, where she works to make her ancestors proud and leave a just, equitable society for her descendants.

Laurel Ann Bogen is a native Angeleno, having lived (for the most part) 15 miles from the hospital where she was born in downtown Los Angeles. She is the author of eleven books of poetry and short fiction including *Psychosis in the Produce Department, The Last Girl in the Land of the Butterflies* and *Do Iguanas Dance Under the Moonlight?* In addition, she is a founding member of the celebrated poetry performance ensemble, Nearly Fatal Women, and taught in the Writer's Program at UCLA Extension for thirty years.

Laure-Anne Bosselaar is the author of *The Hour Between Dog and Wolf*, *Small Gods of Grief*, (Isabella Gardner Prize, 2001) and *of A New Hunger*, an ALA Notable Book. Her latest book, *These Many Rooms*, came out from Four Way Books. The winner of the 2021 James Dickey Poetry Prize, and the recipient of a Pushcart Prize, she edited five anthologies. She is part of the founding faculty at the Solstice Low Residency MFA Program.

Jennifer Bradpiece was born and raised in the multifaceted muse, Los Angeles, where she still resides. Project collaborations with multimedia artists, far and near, feed her passion. Jennifer's poetry has been nominated for a Pushcart Prize and published in various anthologies, journals, and online zines. She is the author of *Lullabies for End Times* (Moon Tide Press, 2020), and *Ophelia on Acid* (Blue Horse Press, 2021).

Bob Branaman - In 1959 Beat Generation poet, painter, sculptor, and filmmaker, Bob Branaman left his hometown in Kansas, and headed west. He presently lives in Southern California where he continues to paint and write. Believing love is all that matters, he has always been an artist, even when he tried not to be.

Gayle Brandeis is the author, most recently, of the novel in poems, Many Restless Concerns (Black Lawrence Press), shortlisted for the Shirley Jackson Award, the memoir, The Art of Misdiagnosis (Beacon Press), and the poetry collection The Selfless Bliss of the Body (Finishing Line Press). Her essay collection Drawing/Breath will be released by Overcup Press in 2023. She teaches in the MFA programs at Sierra Nevada University and Antioch University.

John Brantingham was Sequoia and Kings Canyon National Parks' first poet laureate. His work has been featured in hundreds of magazines, *Writers Almanac* and *The Best Small Fictions 2016*. He has nineteen books of poetry and fiction including *Crossing the High Sierra* (Cholla Needles Press), *California Continuum: Migrations and Amalgamations* (Pelekinesis Press) co-written with Grant Hier and his latest, *Life: Orange to Pear* (Bamboo Dart Press). He teaches at Mt. San Antonio College.

Richard Brautigan (1935 –1984) was a unique and visionary novelist, poet, and short story writer published in the United States, Europe, Japan, and China. Best known for his novels *Trout Fishing in America*, *In Watermelon Sugar*, and *The Abortion: An Historical Romance 1966*, Brautigan's poetry and fiction continues to inspire poets, writers, artists and musicians globally.

Jack Brewer is a musician and poet known for his work as the singer and lyricist for the Los Angeles post-hardcore band Saccharine Trust which he co-founded with guitarist Joe Baiza in 1980. His book of poetry *No Lunch* was published by Sinistry Press in 1991.

Derrick Brown has toured as a poet around the world. He has performed at Glastonbury, All Tomorrow's Parties, Berlin Intl. Lit Festival. He had a poetry book shop in Austin Texas, performed on *The Tonight Show* and is the founder and president of Write Bloody Publishing. He has published nine books of poetry. He runs the Your River Is Waiting workshop series as well as a writing workshop series for fellow veterans.

Eric Brown rode into the universe on a tardigrade and hopes to depart it through the No-Holds-Barred Spin-N-Hit in a flurry of charm quarks.

Charles Bukowski (1920-1994) was born in Andernach, Germany. At the age of three, his family moved to the United States, he grew up in Los Angeles. Bukowski published his first story when he was twenty-four and began writing poetry at the age of thirty-five. His first book of poetry was published in 1959; he went on to publish more than forty-five books of poetry and prose, receiving international acclaim during his lifetime.

Billy Burgos is a poet/painter/designer from Los Angeles. He has always had a hard time choosing which art he is most driven by so he has pursued all three with a similar (pedal to the floor) drive. It is all madness but in the process he has a poetry collection *Eulogy To An Unknown Tree* on Writ Large Press and is working on a new gallery exhibit showcasing his ink drawings.

Ronnie Burk (1955-2003) was a visionary poet, remarkable collagist, and dedicated political activist. In his youth he studied Buddhism and literature at the Naropa Institute in Colorado. Active in the early Chicano movement of the 1970s, he became a leading force in the controversial San Francisco branch of ACT UP, fighting for the rights of people diagnosed with HIV. Burk traveled widely and sought out like-minded friends and mentors, including Allen Ginsberg, Diane di Prima, Charles Henri Ford, and Philip Lamantia.

James Cagney is the author of *Black Steel Magnolias In The Hour Of Chaos Theory*, winner of the PEN Oakland 2018 Josephine Miles Award. His newest book, *Martian: The Saint of Loneliness* is the winner of the 2021 James Laughlin Award from the Academy of American Poets. It is due from Nomadic Press in 2022. For more information, please visit www.JamesCagneypoet.com

Don Kingfisher Campbell, MFA in Creative Writing from Antioch University Los Angeles, taught Writers Seminar at Occidental College Upward Bound for 36 years, been a coach and judge for Poetry Out Loud, a performing poet/teacher for Red Hen Press Youth Writing Workshops, L.A. Coordinator and Board Member of California Poets In The Schools, poetry editor of the *Angel City Review*, publisher of *Spectrum* magazine, and host of the Saturday Afternoon Poetry reading series in Pasadena, California.

Carolyn (Elizabeth Robinson) Cassady (1923-2013). In 1947 while studying towards a Master's Degree in Theater Arts in Denver, Carolyn met Neal Cassady whom she married in 1948, together they had three children. After Neal's imprisonment and parole in 1963, Carolyn divorced him and began her literary life. Her first book, *Heart Beat* was made into a movie starring Sissy Spacek, Nick Nolte and John Heard. In 1983, Carolyn moved to England where she died in 2013. Other titles include *Off the Road, Twenty Years with Cassady, Kerouac and Ginsberg (1990), Travel Tips for the Timid; What Guidebooks Never Tell* (2018) and a book of her poetry, *Poetic Portrait: Carolyn Cassady Revealed in Poetry and Prose (2020)*.

Neal (Leon) Cassady (1926-1968). At 14, Neal began "borrowing" cars spending most of his teen years in and out of reformatories. In 1947, Neal and his first wife, 15-year-old Luanne Henderson, drove to NYC where Neal met Jack Kerouac and Allen Ginsberg. In 1948, after his marriage was annulled, Neal married Carolyn Robinson, together they had three children. In 1958, Neal was arrested for marijuana charges, spending two years in San Quentin Prison. Upon the completion of his parole in 1963, Carolyn divorced him. Neal met author Ken Kesey, participating in the "Acid Tests", becoming the driver of the psychedelically-painted bus, Further. In February 1968, Neal was discovered unconscious lying near railroad tracks leading out of San Miguel de Allende, Mexico. He died the next day, four days before his 42nd birthday.

MK Chavez is an Afro-Latinx writer. She is the author of *Mothermorphosis, Dear Animal,* and *A Brief History of the Selfie.* Chavez curates the reading series Lyrics & Dirges and co-directs the Berkeley Poetry Festival, a recipient of Alameda County Arts Leadership Award, the PEN Oakland Josephine Miles Award, and the 2021 San Francisco Foundation/Nomadic Press literary award. Her most recent work can be found in the Academy of Poets Poem-A-Day series and Golden Gate Park in San Francisco with the Voice of Trees projects.

Neeli Cherkovski has written biographies of Lawrence Ferlinghetti and Charles Bukowski, with whom he co-edited the L.A. zine *Laugh Literary and Man the Humping Guns.* Poetry critic Gerald Nicosia said of Cherkovski: "...in the end, what stamps Cherkovski's poetry as unique is its unbounded lyrical gift easily greater than that of any other poet of his generation." His body of poetry includes *Elegy for Bob Kaufman* and *Leaning Against Time,* for which he was awarded the 15th Annual PEN Oakland/Josephine Miles Literary Award in 2005.

Renown L.A. poet **Wanda Coleman** (1946-2013) grew up in the Watts neighborhood. During her lifetime she worked as a medical secretary, magazine editor, journalist, and Emmy Award-winning scriptwriter before turning to poetry. Her collection *Mercurochrome: New Poems (2001)* was a finalist for the National Book Award in poetry. The poet Juan Felipe Herrera called Coleman the "word-caster of live coals of Watts & LA." A recipient of fellowships from the NEA and the Guggenheim Foundation, Coleman was regarded as a central L.A. literary figure. The *Los Angeles Times* book critic David Ulin noted that Coleman, "helped transform the city's literature."

Larry Colker (1947-2018) had been a staple in the Southern California poetry community before his passing. He ran the Redondo Poets Reading Series at the Coffee Cartel in Redondo Beach, was the webmaster for Poetix, Southern California's poetry event clearing house, and led the Wednesday Night Poetry Workshop at Beyond Baroque in Venice, CA, where he also served as a Board member. He is missed.

Brendan Constantine is the author of several collections of poetry, among them 'Letters to Guns' (2009) and 'Close Call' (2022). His work has appeared in *Poetry, The Nation, Best American Poetry, Poetry Daily, Tin House,* and *Poem-a-Day*, among other journals. A popular performer, Constantine has presented his work to audiences throughout the U.S. and Europe, also appearing on TED ED, NPR's All Things Considered. He currently teaches at the Windward School in west Los Angeles.

Kitty Costello worked 30 years for the San Francisco Public Library and as a psychotherapist. Diane di Prima was among her root teachers. She has released the poetry collection, *Upon Waking: New & Selected Poems 1977-2017*, and coedited *Muslim American Writers at Home: Stories, Essays & Poems of Identity, Diversity & Belonging.* She is literary executor for Indigenous Alaskan writer Mary TallMountain and serves on the board of Freedom Voices, a press with the mission of publishing works that speak to and from communities on the margins.

Peter Coyote was one of the founders of the Diggers, an S.F. anarchist improv group active during the 1960s. Many of Coyote's stories from the counter-culture period are included in his memoir, *Sleeping Where I Fall.* Coyote is also a prominent actor, writer, and director. His memoir *The Rainman's Third Cure: An Irregular Education* "provides portraits of mentors that shaped him—including his violent, intimidating father, a bass player, a Mafia Consiglieri, and beat poet Gary Snyder, who introduced him to the practice of Zen."

Originally from Stockton, California, **Annette Cruz** has resided in North East LA since 1974. She has performed her poetry in various LA venues ranging from Beyond Baroque, The World Stage, Library Girl, Avenue 50 Studio and Timothy Leary's final birthday party at his home in the Hollywood Hills. After going into hiatus in 2002 to concentrate on raising her youngest son, she has now re-emerged with conviction and purpose and is writing her first book.

Dennis Cruz has been writing and performing his poetry for over 20 years. He has been published in anthologies as well as online publications including *THE CHIRON REVIEW*, the Nervous Breakdown, *Crush* Fan Zine, and *Sensitive Skin* Magazine. He has lectured at the USC Community Literature Incentive, the Harvard-Westlake preparatory school, as well the LA county Jail for men AND women. His latest collection of Poems, *THE BEAST IS WE*, is available from PUNK HOSTAGE PRESS.

King Daddy writes poems in black notebooks. He has been a member of the performance poetry troupe Poets in Distress for 25 years. He is practically unpublished and has won no awards or prizes.

Born in 1954 in a small town on the shores of Caspian Sea, **Soheyl Dahi** has lived in the San Francisco Bay Area since 1979. He is a poet, painter and publisher of Sore Dove Press since 1986. These days, he quietly writes and paints in a small room in his basement, interrupted occasionally by a Coyote who stops and looks at him curiously through the window.

Cassandra Dallett has published multiple chapbooks and full-length poetry collections, two of which—*On Sunday* and *A Finch and Collapse* (Nomadic Press)—were nominated for CA Book awards. She has been nominated for six Pushcarts and was recently in the running for Oakland's first Poet Laureate. Dallett has graced many stages, hosts the weekly writing workshop ON TWO SIX, The Badass Bookworm Podcast, and The Badass Bookworm's Lit Loft. Her most recent poetry collection, *A Pretty Little Wilderness*, was released in June 2020 (Be About It Press).

Nicelle Davis is a poet, collaborator, and performance artist. Her poetry collections include *The Walled Wife* (Red Hen Press, 2016), *In the Circus of You* (Rose Metal Press, 2015), *Becoming Judas* (Red Hen Press, 2013), and *Circe* (Lowbrow Press, 2011). Her poetry film collaborations with Cheryl Gross have been shown internationally. She has taught poetry at Youth for Positive Change, MHA, Volunteers of America, and with Red Hen's WITS program. She is the creator of The Poetry Circus and currently teaches at Knight High School.

Poet **Yvonne De La Vega** (1959-2019) was born and raised in Los Angeles. Her voice is one of social consciousness, personal mythos, and cultural compassion. Yvonne has recorded spoken-word projects with music and recording industry luminaries such as Ray Manzarek of The Doors and Herb Alpert (A&M Records). She appears on Malcolm McClaren's *Round The Outside, Round The Outside* album (Virgin Records), with a poem by Garcia Lorca. She has also been featured on several spoken word recordings produced by Harvey Kubernik.

Kathryn de Lancellotti's chapbook *Impossible Thirst* was published June 2020, Moon Tide Press. She is a Pushcart Prize nominee and a former recipient of the George Hitchcock Memorial Poetry Prize. Her poems and other works have appeared in *Thrush, Rust + Moth, The American Journal of Poetry, Quarterly West*, and others. She received her MFA in Creative Writing from Sierra Nevada University and resides on the Central Coast, California, with her family.

Natasha Dennerstein was born in Melbourne, Australia. She has an MFA from San Francisco State University. Her collections *Anatomize* (2015), *Triptych Caliform* (2016) and novella-in-verse *About a Girl* (2017) were published by Norfolk Press. Her trans chapbook *Seahorse* (2017) was published by Nomadic Press. She lives in Oakland, where she is an editor at Nomadic Press and works at St James Infirmary, a clinic for sex-workers in San Francisco. She was a 2018 Fellow of the Lambda Literary Writer's Retreat.

Diane di Prima (1934–2020). Brooklyn-born. Fledged in the Beat era in Greenwich Village. Revolutionary community organizer with the Diggers in San Francisco. Her book of poems, *Revolutionary Letters*, was anthem and instruction manual for the Sixties. Founder and editor of numerous presses. Her book-length poem *Loba* was a talisman, a feast of female archetypes for the women's movement. A Tibetan Buddhist. Mother of five. Teacher of poetics at Naropa in Boulder and New College in SF. Poet Laureate of San Francisco. And so much more….

Peggy Dobreer is a three-time pushcart nominated poet and recipient of the 2017 Poetry Matters Prize. She has released two full length collections with Moon Tide Press, *In the Lake of Your Bones* 2012 and *Drop & Dazzle* 2018. Her most recent chapbook, *Forbidden Plums*, was published by Glass Lyre Press, Chicago. Peggy curates Slow Lightning online and is a Community of Writers facilitator assisting Janet Fitch. She is a member of Beyond Baroque and the Long Now Foundation. Link and further information at www.peggydobreer.com.

Kim Dower has published four highly-acclaimed collections of poetry: *Air Kissing on Mars, Slice of Moon, Last Train to the Missing Planet*, and *Sunbathing on Tyrone Power's Grave*. Her newest, *I Wore This Dress Today for You, Mom*, will be published in April, 2022. Her poems have been widely anthologized and nominated for several Pushcarts. Former Poet Laureate of West Hollywood, Kim teaches poetry workshops for Antioch University, The West Hollywood Library, UCLA Extension, and the Los Angeles LGBT Center. www.kimdowerpoetry.com.

Elisabeth Adwin Edwards's poems have appeared in *The Tampa Review, Rust + Moth, Tinderbox Poetry Journal, The American Journal of Poetry, A-Minor Magazine*, and elsewhere; her prose appears in *Hobart, CutBank, On The Seawall*, and other publications. Her work has been nominated for Best of the Net and a Pushcart Prize. She lives in Los Angeles with her husband and teen daughter in an apartment filled with books.

L.A. poet **Alexis Rhone Fancher's** six collections include *The Dead Kid Poems (KYSO Flash Press)* and *Junkie Wife (Moon Tide Press)*. *EROTIC: New & Collected*, from *New York Quarterly*, dropped in March, 2021. She's published in *Best American Poetry, Plume, Diode, The American Journal of Poetry, Spillway, Hobart, Gargoyle, Cleaver, Nashville Review*, and elsewhere. Her photos are published worldwide. Alexis is poetry editor of *Cultural Daily*.
Find her at www.alexisrhonefancher.com

Pushcart-nominated poet **Rich Ferguson** has shared the stage with Patti Smith, Wanda Coleman, and other esteemed poets and musicians. Ferguson has been selected by the National Beat Poetry Foundation, Inc. to serve as the State of California Beat Poet Laureate (Sept. 2020 to Sept. 2022). He is featured in the film, *What About Me?* including Michael Stipe, Michael Franti, and others. His latest poetry collection, *Everything Is Radiant Between the Hates*, has been released by Moon Tide Press.

Lawrence Ferlinghetti (1919-2021) was an internationalist poet, painter and publisher. He was an eye-witness to a Century and did his part to fight for freedom of speech, not just in his own country but around the world. His 'howl' continues to be heard.

Jamie Asaye FitzGerald is a Los Angeles mixed race/hapa poet from Hawai'i with work in journals and anthologies, including *The American Poetry Review, Works & Days* and *Mom Egg Review*. She earned an MFA in poetry from San Diego State University and a BA in English/Creative Writing from the University of Southern California. For over a decade, she has worked for *Poets & Writers* in its Los Angeles office.

Bob Flanagan (1952-1996) was a poet, musician and performance artist known for his public performances incorporating his lifelong struggle with cystic fibrosis. Long running director of Beyond Baroque's Wednesday night poetry workshop, Bob's final years were portrayed in a documentary film released the year after his death, *SICK: The Life & Death of Bob Flanagan, Supermasochist.*

Michael C Ford's debut 12-inch-vinyl recording *Language Commando* earned a Grammy nomination on the 1st ballot in 1986 and his book of selected work: *Emergency Exits* earned initial nomination for the Pulitzer Prize short list in 1998. *Populated Wilderness* was published in a 2020 chapbook format as a fundraiser for the Lockwood Animal Rescue Center. Daniel J. Yaryan under his Mystic Boxing Commission imprint will be marketing a book-length publication of MCF's most recent title *In Case of Flood Stand on this Book – It's Dry English.*

francEyE (1922-2009) often referred to as "the female Charles Bukowski," was born Frances Elizabeth Dean in San Rafael, California. A winner of the Allen J. Freedman Poetry Prize, francEyE is the author of *Snaggletooth In Ocean Park* (Sacred Beverage Press, 1996), *Amber Spider* (Pearl Editions, 2004), *Grandma Stories* (Conflux Press, 2008) and *Call* (Rose of Sharon Press, 2009). francEyE's eclectic past includes a tour of duty in the Women's Army Corps during World War II and a stint during the 1970s as a waitress at Al's Kitchen on the Santa Monica Pier.

Poet, editor, publisher, and Pushcart nominee **Amélie Frank** has authored five poetry collections and one spoken word CD. Her work has appeared in *Art/Life, Lummox, Poeticdiversity, Sparring with Beatnik Ghosts, Levure littéraire, Cultural Weekly, Wide Awake, 1001 Knights,* and *Voices From Leimert Park Redux.* Beyond Baroque Literary/Arts Center and the cities of Venice and Los Angeles have honored her for her activism and leadership in the Southern California poetry community.

Allen J. Freedman (1942-1993) was regular at the Water Espresso Gallery Wednesday night open readings in Hollywood, CA. in the mid-80s. Later Allen would a be a major player at the Iguana Café poetry scene in N. Hollywood, CA. To honor his memory and his commitment to poetry, the Allen J. Freedman Memorial Poetry Prize was created and presented annually for many years.

Nelson Gary's works include *XXX, Cinema, A Wonderful Life in Our Lives: Sketches of a Honeymoon in Mexico, Twin Volumes,* and *Pharmacy Psalms and Half-Life Hymns—for Nothing*. He is an award-winning poet and essayist. He is a Beyond Baroque Fellow who recorded his poetry with Elliott Smith.

Frank X. Gaspar is the author of five collections of poetry and two novels. Among his many awards are multiple inclusions in Best American Poetry, four Pushcart Prizes, and a National Endowment for the Arts Fellowship in Literature. His debut novel, *Leaving Pico*, was a Barnes and Noble Discovery Prize winner, and a *New York Times* Notable Book. His second novel, *Stealing Fatima*, was a MassBook of the Year in Fiction). His work has appeared widely in serial publications.

Pleasant Gehman is multi-talented: she's a dancer, actor, musician, visual artist and Tarot reader. She is the author of nine books, including *Showgirl Confidential: My Life Onstage, Backstage And On The Road* (2013) and *Rock & Roll Witch: A Memoir Of Sex Magick, Drugs And Rock & Roll* (2021), both published by Punk Hostage Press.

Amy Gerstler's most recent book of poems is *Index of Women* (Penguin Random House, 2021). Her work has appeared in a variety of magazines and anthologies. She is currently collaborating with composer, actor, and arranger Steve Gunderson on a musical play. Her previous books of poems include *Scattered at Sea, Dearest Creature, Ghost Girl, Medicine, Crown of Weeds, Nerve Storm,* and *Bitter Angel*. She has also written fiction, nonfiction, and journalism and art criticism.

Charlie Getter was originally fashioned out of the mud of the west bank of the Vltava River in 1620, during the short reign of Frederick, King of Bohemia and Elector of the Palatinate. He has been dissolved and reconstituted and re-vivified many times by various rabbinical scholars, his last iteration initiated on the eastern seaboard of North America sometime after the "Summer of Love." He is rumored to be in San Francisco, but rumors are scarcely worth the air spent to breathe them...

Kelly Gray (she/her/hers) is a writer and educator living on occupied Coast Miwok land, deep in fire country. She is the author of the poetry collection *Instructions for an Animal Body* (Moon Tide Press) and the audio chapbook *My Fingers are Whales* (Moon Child Press). Her writing appears or is forthcoming in *Passages North, Pithead Chapel, Hobart, Under a Warm Green Linden, The Normal School, The Inflectionist, Barren Magazine, Lunch Ticket, Superstition Review* and elsewhere. You can read more of her work at www.writekgray.com.

S.A. Griffin lives, loves, and works in Los Angeles.

Q.R. Hand Jr. (1937-2020) was the author of four poetry books, i speak to the poet in man (jukebox press, 1985), how sweet it is (Zeitgeist Press, 1996), whose really blues, new & selected poems (Taurean Horn Press, 2007), and the posthumous *Out of Nothing*. He was a member of the poetry and jazz ensemble Wordwind Chorus and worked as a community mental health worker in San Francisco, where he lived for more than four decades.

Robert Hass is a poet, essayist, and translator. His most recent book is *Summer Snow: New Poems* (Ecco Press). He is a professor of English emeritus at the University of California at Berkeley.

A fixture in the Los Angeles literary community for over thirty years, **Susan Hayden** is a poet, playwright, novelist and essayist. She is the creator, curator and producer of the long-running series Library Girl, a monthly words and music event now in its 13th year at Ruskin Group Theatre. In 2015, Hayden was presented with the Bruria Finkel/Artist In The Community Award from Santa Monica Arts Foundation for her "significant contributions to the energetic discourse within Santa Monica's arts community."

Jack Hirschman (1933-2021) Overtly and unapologetically political, Jack was a Marxist-Stalinist and fiercely American poet with over 75 books to his credit. A fearless activist for many progressive causes, he devoted his life to the advancement of poetry. Fluent in Italian and French Jack translated poetry from over a dozen languages. In 2006, he was appointed the Poet Laureate for the City of San Francisco using that position to inaugurate an International Poetry Festival by inviting poets from Canada to Palestine to Albania to come to San Francisco.

Jane Hirshfield's ninth poetry collection, *Ledger* (Knopf, 2020), centers on the crises of biosphere and social justice. Other books include two now-classic books of essays, *Nine Gates* and *Ten Windows*. Hirshfield has received the Poetry Center and California Book Awards, fellowships from the Guggenheim and Rockefeller foundations and NEA, and ten selections for *The Best American Poetry*. Lay ordained in Soto Zen, Hirshfield is a 2019 elected member of the American Academy of Arts & Sciences.

Tanya (Hyonhye) Ko Hong is a bilingual Korean American poet, translator, playwright, and cultural curator. She has an MFA in Creative Writing from Antioch University L.A. Tanya was the first Korean-American recipient of the Yun Doon-ju Korean-American Literature Award and the 10th Ko Won Memorial Foundation Literature Award in 2020. Her segmented poem, "Comfort Woman," won the 11th Moon Prize from *Writing in a Woman's Voice*; it is now being turned into a play. She splits her time in L.A. and NYC.

Jimmy Jazz is a writer from San Diego. He is the author of *The Sub, The Cadillac Tramps, The Book of Books* & *M-Theory*. In 2022, he released a poetry collection called *Nothing a Fire Can't Fix*.

Luke Johnson lives on the California coast with his wife and three kids. His poems can be found at *Kenyon Review, Narrative Magazine, Florida Review, Frontier, Cortland Review, Nimrod, Thrush* and elsewhere. His manuscript in progress was recently named a finalist for the Jake Adam York Prize, The Levis through Four Way Press, The Vassar Miller Award and is forthcoming fall 2023 from Texas Review Press. You can find more of his poetry at www.lukethepoet.com or connect at Twitter at @Lukesrant.

Bob Kaufman (1925-1986) was an African-American poet and key figure of the Beat movement. At 13 he joined the U.S. Merchant Marine, sailing around the globe nine times. Settling in San Francisco in 1958, he was a cofounder of *Beatitude*. After the assassination of President John F. Kennedy in 1963, Kaufman took a vow of silence, neither speaking nor writing, until the end of the Vietnam War. Afterwards he wrote prolifically. In 1978 resumed his silence, which he broke rarely for the rest of his life. *The Collected Poems of Bob Kaufman* were published by City Lights Books in 2019.

Douglas Kearney has published seven books ranging from poetry to essays to libretti. His seventh book, *Sho*, was a National Book Award finalist. He is the 2021 recipient of OPERA America's Campbell Opera Librettist Prize, created and generously funded by librettist/lyricist Mark Campbell. A Whiting Writer's and Foundation for Contemporary Arts Cy Twombly awardee with residencies/fellowships from Cave Canem, The Rauschenberg Foundation, and others. He teaches Creative Writing at the University of Minnesota–Twin Cities.

E.K. Keith is a Latinx poet in San Francisco, and *Ordinary Villains* (Nomadic Press, 2018) is her first book. Type her name in any search bar to enjoy her poetry published online and videos of her performances. Please do more work to bring about environmental and racial justice.

Doug Knott has written and performed poetry in Southern California since the 80s. He is the author of the collection, *Small Dogs Bark Cartoons*, many chapbooks and several poetry videos. He has performed his poetry nationally, and was board president of Beyond Baroque Literary Foundation in LA for 4 years.

Ron Koertge has the usual collection of publications and awards. Modesty prevents a long, stunning list.

Joanne Kyger (1934-2017), associated with the San Francisco Renaissance, the Beat Generation, Black Mountain, and the New York School was the author of over 30 books of poetry and prose. In a 2007 review of Kyger's book *About Now: Collected Poems*, Lewis MacAdams describes Kyger as from the "School of Backyard Poets, who look out their kitchen windows and see the universe."

Philip Lamantia (1927-2005) was born in San Francisco, son of Sicilian immigrants. At age 15, he was first published in surrealist journals in New York. He played a prominent role in the San Francisco Renaissance and the Beat Generation, and sought adventure, living in Spain, Morocco, and Mexico. He helped to revive the visionary tradition of romanticism, drawing on mystical and hallucinatory drug experiences. An impassioned seeker of knowledge, he wrote poetry at once ecstatic, anguished, demanding, and bold.

Dorianne Laux's 6th collection, *Only As the Day is Long: New & Selected Poems* was a finalist for the 2020 Pulitzer Prize for Poetry. She is the winner of the Paterson Prize for *The Book of Men*, and The Oregon Book Award for *Facts About the Moon*, which was also short-listed for the Lenore Marshall Poetry Prize. Laux is also the author of *Awake: What We Carry*, a finalist for the National Book Critic's Circle Award; *Smoke*, and *The Book of Women*. She is the co-author of the celebrated text *The Poet's Companion: A Guide to the Pleasures of Writing Poetry*.

Gary Lemons published 8 books of poetry with his newest book—*Spell*—scheduled with Red Hen Press in 2024. He has a BFA from U of Iowa Poetry Workshop and studied with among others Diane Wakowski, John Berryman, Marvin Bell, Donald Justice, William Stafford, Maxine Kumin and particularly Norman Dubie.

Philip Levine (1928 – 2015) born and raised in Detroit, Michigan, Levine was an American poet best known for his poems about working-class Detroit. He taught for more than thirty years in the English department of California State University, Fresno and held teaching positions at other universities as well. He served on the Board of Chancellors of the Academy of American Poets from 2000 to 2006 and was appointed Poet Laureate of the United States for 2011–2012. Among his many accolades, in 1995 he was awarded the Pulitzer Prize in Poetry for *The Simple Truth*.

La Loca, nee Pamala Karol, is a self-described "poetess/philanderer." She was one of four American writers chosen to represent the United States in the 1988 Winter Olympics Arts Festival in Calgary, Canada. La Loca grew up in impoverished Chicano districts of Los Angeles, and now lives in Hollywood, California.

Ellaraine Lockie's recent work has won both the Oprelle Publishing's Poetry Masters Contest and their Bigger Than Me Contest Award, the Poetry Super Highway Contest, and others. Her chapbook collections have won Poetry Forum's Chapbook Contest Prize, San Gabriel Valley Poetry Festival Chapbook Competition, Encircle Publications Chapbook Contest, Best Individual Poetry Collection Award from Purple Patch magazine in England, and The Aurorean's Chapbook Choice Award. Ellaraine teaches writing workshops and serves as Poetry Editor for the lifestyles magazine, *LILIPOH*.

Gerald Locklin (1941-2021) was a Professor Emeritus of English at California State University, Long Beach, where he taught from 1965 through 2007, and continued as an occasional part-time lecturer. A profile based on a retirement event was broadcast on NPR and is archived. He was the author of over 155 books, chapbooks, and broadsides of poetry, fiction, and criticism, with over 3000 poems, stories, articles, reviews, and interviews published in periodicals. His work is frequently performed by Garrison Keillor on his *Writer's Almanac* daily Public Radio program, is archived on his website, and is included in all three of Mr. Keillor's *Good Poems* anthologies. His most recent full-length collections of poems were *Poets and Pleasure Seekers*, Spout Hill Press, 2015, and *The Marriage of Man the Maker and Mother Nature, Volume 2 of the Complete Coagula Art Poems*, 2014. Gerald Locklin died from Covid 19 in 2021. He was 79.

Beat legend **Philomene Long** (1940-2007) was born in Greenwich Village and cut her literary teeth listening to poets verbally sear the paint off the walls of their private hells. Later, after escaping a five-year sentence in a Los Angeles convent, she migrated to Venice, wrote poems and was crowned "Queen of Bohemia." Poet and film director, her films include *The Beats: An Existential Comedy* and *The California Missions*. Her many books include *American Zen Bones* (Beyond Baroque Books, 1999) and *The Collected Poems of Philomene Long* (Raven Productions, 2010).

Jessica Loos is a poet, event organizer, performer, & collage artist who lives in North Beach, San Francisco.

Richard Loranger is a multi-genre writer, performer, visual artist, and all-around squeaky wheel, currently residing in Oakland, CA. He is the founder of Poetea, a monthly literary conversation group. His newest book *Unit of Agency* is just out from Collapse Press in October, 2021. He's also the author of *Be A Bough Tit, Sudden Windows, Poems for Teeth, The Orange Book*, and ten chapbooks, and has work in over 100 magazines and journals. You can find out more at www.richardloranger.com.

Suzanne Lummis' poetry has appeared in *Spillway, Ploughshares, New Ohio Review, Plume, The American Journal of Poetry, The New Yorker*. Her essay-memoir "Some Notes on Death" is in the new What Books anthology, *What Falls Away is Always*. She's published three collections; *Open 24 Hours* received the Blue Lynx Prize. She was a 2018/19 COLA (City of Los Angeles) fellow, an endowment to influential artists, writers and musicians to create new bodies of work. Poetry.la producers her YouTube noir-themed series, *They Write by Night*.

Rick Lupert has been involved with poetry since 1990. A Pushcart Prize and Best of the Net nominee, he created PoetrySuperHighway.com and hosts the weekly Virtual Cobalt Cafe series). His 25 collections of poetry, include "God Wrestler" and "The Tokyo-Van Nuys Express." He edited the anthologies "A Poet's Siddur", "A Poet's Haggadah", "The Night Goes on All Night." and "Ekphrastia Gone Wild." He works as a music teacher and graphic designer in Los Angeles.

Lewis MacAdams (1944-2020) was born in West Texas in 1944. He graduated from Princeton and also attended S.U.N.Y. Buffalo. He lived in Bolinas, California from 1970 to 1980 and was the director of the Poetry Center at San Francisco State University from 1975 to 1978. He moved to Los Angeles in 1980 and was the founder of Friends of the Los Angeles River. He published over a dozen books of poetry. Macadams died in 2020 due to complications from Parkinson's disease.

Phoebe MacAdams was born New York, but has mostly lived in California, moving to LA in 1986. With the poets James Cushing, the late Holly Prado and Harry Northup, she is a founding member of Cahuenga Press, which published five of her eight books, including her new and selected volume, *The Large Economy of the Beautiful*. She taught English at Roosevelt High School in Boyle Heights until her retirement in 2011. She lives in Pasadena with her husband, Ron Ozuna.

Sarah Maclay's *Nightfall Marginalia* is due out in 2023, from What Books. Other recent collections include *The "She" Series: A Venice Correspondence*, with Holaday Mason, and *Music for the Black Room* (UT Press). Her work has appeared in *APR, FIELD, Ploughshares, The Best American Erotic Poetry, The Writer's Chronicle, Poetry International,* and beyond. A recipient of a COLA Fellowship, a Pushcart special mention, the Tampa Review Prize for Poetry, and a Yaddo residency, she teaches at LMU and conducts workshops at Beyond Baroque.

devorah major is an American writer, editor, recording artist, and professor. She has won awards in poetry, fiction, and creative non-fiction and is San Francisco's third Poet Laureate Emerita.

William J. Margolis (1927-1998) Born in Chicago, served in the U.S. Navy, moved to San Francisco, an active participant in North Beach and Venice West poetry scenes. In addition to *Beatitude*, he edited *The Miscellaneous Man, Mendicant,* and *Miscellaneous Man: The New Los Angeles Quarterly of Literature & Art*. In 1959, Margolis fell from a second story window in his San Francisco apartment, impaling himself on a fire hydrant. He remained wheelchair bound for the remainder of his life.

Clint Margrave is the author of the novel *Lying Bastard* (Run Amok Books, 2020), and the poetry collections, *Salute the Wreckage*, *The Early Death of Men*, and *Visitor* (Forthcoming) all from NYQ Books. His work has appeared in *The Threepenny Review*, *Rattle*, and *The Moth*, among others. He lives in Los Angeles, CA.

Milo Martin is a Californian spoken word poet who was an integral spark in the now-legendary bohemian ONYX literary scene in East Hollywood of the mid/late 90s. He co-founded the Hollywood slam team who went on to win two national titles. Progenitor of the Utopian Nihilists, his lineage to the Beats runs deep meeting with Ginsberg, di Prima, Micheline, Aram Saroyan, Bill Minor, and Amiri Baraka. He has toured Europe five times with POESIE UNITED, the first and only international spoken word poetry troupe of its kind.

Tongo Eisen-Martin is an educator and organizer whose work centers on issues of mass incarceration, extrajudicial killings of Black people, and human rights. He has taught at detention centers around the country and at the Institute for Research in African-American Studies at Columbia University. He is the 8th Poet Laureate of San Francisco.

Clive Matson (MFA Columbia University 1989) writes from the itch in his body and that's old hat, according to his tutorial *Let the Crazy Child Write!* (1998). Beat Generation writers were his teachers in the 1960s and he immersed himself in deep passions that run through us all. He taught creative writing at UC Berkeley Extension and now, after finishing *Hello, Paradise. Paradise, Goodbye*, he helps students set up WordSwell.xyz (which see), founded on the pre-Modernist principles that spawned the Beats.

Ellyn Maybe, Southern California based poet, United States Artist nominee 2012, is the author of numerous books and widely anthologized. She has a critically acclaimed album, *Rodeo for the Sheepish* (Hen House Studios). Her latest poetry/music project is called ellyn & robbie. Their album, *Skywriting with Glitter*, has also received high praise. She also has forthcoming collaborative poetry projects with Joshua Corwin including *Ghosts Sing into the World's Ear*.

Stephen Meadows is a Californian of Ohlone Indian and pioneer descent. One of his poems graces a bronze plaque in the city of San Francisco. Stephen is a folk music DJ at KFOK Community Radio and holds a Master's Degree from San Francisco State University. He lives with his wife and son in the foothills of the Sierra Nevada. His second solo book *Winter Work* will be published by Nomadic Press in 2022.

David Meltzer, poet, editor, publisher, musician, and educator, David Meltzer authored many volumes of poetry, fiction, and essays, including "When I Was A Poet", # 60 in City Lights' Pocket Poets Series. Pureland Audio released his last CD, "Two-Tone Poetry & Jazz", recorded with poet Julie Rogers, and saxophonist Zan Stewart. Recent books are *Trading Fours* and *Sharing Breath*, and forthcoming is *Rock Tao* published by Lithic Press.

Ann Menebroker (1936-2016) was a poet and a longtime resident of Sacramento with over 20 published chapbooks and countless appearances in anthologies. An early friend and correspondent of Charles Bukowski, Ann was part of a group of poets that became known as 'Meat Poets'. Some of their letters were published in the three volumes of Bukowski's letters by Black Sparrow Press.

Jack Micheline (1929-1998) was of Russian-Romanian ancestry and worked as a union organizer before dedicating his life to poetry and painting. He moved to Greenwich Village in the 1950s, where he became a street poet, drawing on jazz, Harlem blues, and the cadence of word rhythms. In 1957, Troubadour Press published his first book *River of Red Wine*; Jack Kerouac wrote the introduction. Micheline relocated to San Francisco in the early 60s, where he spent the rest of his life, eventually publishing over 20 books.

Joseph Millar's *Dark Harvest: New and Selected Poems* is just out from Carnegie Mellon. His work has won fellowships from the NEA and the Guggenheim Foundation. He teaches in Pacific University's low residency MFA.

Richard Modiano is a native of Los Angeles. From 2010 to 2019, he served as Executive Director of Beyond Baroque Literary/Arts Center. In that time he produced and curated hundreds of literary events. Richard is a rank and file member of the Industrial Workers of the World. In 2019 he was elected Vice President of the California State Poetry Society. The Huffington Post named him as one of 200 people doing the most to promote poetry in the United States. His collection *The Forbidden Lunchbox* is published by Punk Hostage Press.

Bill Mohr is a professor in English at California State University, Long Beach. *Holdouts: The Los Angeles Poetry Renaissance 1948-1992*, was published by the University of Iowa Press in 2011. His most recent collection of poems, *The Headwaters of Nirvana / Los Manantiales del Nirvana*, is a bilingual edition published in 2018 by What Books in Los Angeles as an expansion of the Bonobos Editores version published in Mexico in 2015. He blogs at www.billmohrpoet.com; his website is www.koankinship.com.

mike m mollett, It's the Covid era mask & paranoia daze. What's an irreverent art poet Dada/Flux type guy to say now who's lived ¾ a century in Los Angeles? Well, but, really, just tryin' to maintain immediate life & continue to live here, scribble & scratch some texts, weave some art to breathe. I won't give up & sour completely in this fucked-up but wonderful world. Traditionally, I'll state that a new collab publication with Michael Lane Bruner is now available for the adventurous: *Hard to Say in A Way That Might Be Heard* (Rose of Sharon Press, 2021).

Dr. Mongo (1940-2019) poet and performance artist, Dr. Mongo organized poetry events at many Los Angeles venues over the fifty plus years he lived in L.A. and was the poet in residence at Al's Bar at the American Hotel. In the early '60s he introduced poetry readings at the Fifth Estate Coffee House in Hollywood, and for The Los Angeles Free Press, the first underground newspaper in the United States.

Eric Morago is a poet who believes performance carries as much importance on the page as it does off. He is the author of *What We Ache For* and *Feasting on Sky*. Currently Eric is editor-in-chief and publisher of Moon Tide Press. He has an MFA in Creative Writing from California State University, Long Beach, and lives in Los Angeles, CA.

Jim Morrison (1943-1971) is remembered as a filmmaker, poet, singer/songwriter and co-founding member of one of the most emblematic quartets in the history of 20th Century music. Three of JDM's literary documents: *The Lords* and *The New Creatures* printed privately in 1969. followed by *American Prayer* in 1970. Since then, several posthumous trade editions of these and other titles have been Internationally marketed and distributed.

K.R. Morrison is a San Francisco high school teacher, drummer, and poet who is currently on a writing sabbatical in a place she calls "Mermaid Town" in Southern California. Morrison's first collection *Cauldrons* was recently published by Paper Press Books and featured by various podcasts and curations. She is currently a Pushcart nominee for her poem, "Her Altar." Morrison's work has appeared in publications such as *Switchback, Quiet Lightning, Haight Ashbury Literary Journal*, and *Great Weather for Media*.

Henry Mortensen is a film-maker, writer, actor, and musician. He works as an editor at Perceval Press, a small publishing company based in Santa Monica, making books and records. He directed and filmed the music documentary, Skating Polly: Ugly Pop, currently making its way around film festivals.

Briana Muñoz is a Poet from Southern California. She is the author of Loose Lips, a poetry collection published by Prickly Pear Publishing (2019) and of *Everything is Returned to the Soil* published by Flower Song Press (2021). She has performed poetry in places like UNEAC (The National Union of Writers and Artists of Cuba), CECUT (The Tijuana Cultural Center), El Centro Cultural de la Raza in San Diego and beyond.

Majid Naficy, the Arthur Rimbaud of Persian poetry, fled Iran in 1983, a year and a half after the execution of his wife, Ezzat in Tehran. Since 1984 Majid has been living in West Los Angeles. He has published three collections of poetry as well as his doctoral dissertation *Modernism and Ideology in Persian Literature: A Return to Nature in the Poetry of Nima Yushij*.

Greer Nakadegawa-Lee is 17 years old and a senior at Oakland Technical High School. She has written a poem every day for nearly three years now, and she was the 2020 Oakland Youth Poet Laureate. Her first chapbook, "A Heart Full of Hallways" is out now with Nomadic Press.

Johnette Napolitano is an American singer, songwriter and multi-instrumentalist best known as the former lead vocalist/songwriter for the band Concrete Blonde. As the Joshua Tree Recording Company, she regularly collaborates remotely from her desert studio with artists from all over the world. "Exquisite Corpses" is available on CD & vinyl from Schoolkids Records, and the podcast 'Coffee & A Card' can be downloaded from all the usual sources. Contact: joshuatreerecordingcompany@gmail.com

Christine No is a Korean American poet, filmmaker and daughter of immigrants. She is a Sundance Alum, VONA Fellow, Pushcart Prize and Best of the Net Nominee. She has served as Assistant Features Editor for The Rumpus, a Program Coordinator for VONA; and currently serves on the board of Quiet Lightning, a literary nonprofit in the Bay Area. Her first full length poetry collection *Whatever Love Means* is available via Barrelhouse Books. She lives in Oakland with her dog Ruthie Wagmore.

Linda Noel is a California native of the Kooyungkowi people from the northern Sierra. She has a chapbook titled "Where You First Saw the Eyes of Coyote" and has been published in a variety of anthologies and magazines. She has a poem included in the permanent collection at the Autry Museum of the West and another has been adapted and performed by the Pasadena Choir. She has read her work throughout the county. She is a past Poet Laureate of Ukiah, CA.

Harold Norse (1916-2009) raised in Brooklyn, was a member of the bohemian milieu of WWII Greenwich Village that included James Baldwin and W.H. Auden. While living in Paris at the Beat Hotel, Norse participated in the development of Cut Up writing with William Burroughs and Brion Gysin and began a decade-long correspondence with Charles Bukwoski. Norse moved to San Francisco becoming a key figure in Gay Liberation poetry. His collected poems, *In the Hub of the Fiery Force*, were published in 2003. A limited edition of previously unpublished poems, Bozo Emergency, was published by PachinkoPOPPress in 2018.

Harry E. Northup has had twelve books of poetry published: *Amarillo Born, the jon voight poems, Eros Ash, Enough the Great Running Chapel, the images we possess kill the capturing, The Ragged Vertical, Reunions, Greatest Hits, 1996-2001, Red Snow Fence, Where Bodies Again Recline, East Hollywood: Memorial to Reason, Love Poem to MPTF.* He received his B.A. in English from C.S.U.N. where he studied verse with Ann Stanford. Lewis MacAdams, in the L.A. Weekly, wrote, "Northup is the poet laureate of East Hollywood."

Marc Olmsted has appeared in *City Lights Journal, New Directions in Prose & Poetry, New York Quarterly, The Outlaw Bible of American Poetry* and a variety of small presses. He is the author of five collections of poetry, including *What Use Am I a Hungry Ghost?*, which has an introduction by Allen Ginsberg. Olmsted's 25 year relationship with Ginsberg is chronicled in his Beatdom Books memoir *Don't Hesitate: Knowing Allen Ginsberg 1972-1997 - Letters and Recollections*, available on Amazon.

Suzi Kaplan Olmsted has appeared in *The Sun, Maintenant, Big Scream, M.A.G., Lummox Journal,* and *Napalm Health Spa*. She is also one of illustrators of The Ellyn Maybe Coloring Book and the Beatitude Golden Anniversary volume. Nominated for a Pushcart Prize for a poem from her chapbook *Industrial Wallet* (Virgogray Press), she has another chapbook, *Elektra's Mouth*, also on Virgogray. Suzi lives with her husband, poet Marc Olmsted, where they are slaves to the bidding of extraordinary cats Batty and Ellie.

Born and raised in Venice, California, and currently residing in Santa Cruz, **Kevin Opstedal** has written over 25 books of poetry including *Pacific Standard Time* a volume of new and selected poems published by Ugly Duckling Presse in 2016. He is also the editor and publisher of Blue Press Books and has written a literary history of the poets who lived in Bolinas 1968-1980 which was published online by Big Bridge.

Dion O'Reilly's debut book, *Ghost Dogs*, was published in February 2020 by Terrapin Books. Her poems appear in *Cincinnati Review, Poetry Daily, Narrative, The New Ohio Review, The Massachusetts Review, New Letters, Journal of American Poetry, Rattle, The Sun,* and other literary journals and anthologies. She is a member of The Hive Poetry Collective, which produces podcasts and radio shows, and she leads online workshops with poets from all over the United States and Canada.

Joe Pachinko (1960-2017) was born on "Auto Row" in Oakland, California. Arrested for bank robbery at age 17, he held an unusual variety of jobs, including archaeologist, dishwasher, janitor, forklift driver, porno theater bouncer, and Japanese Country & Western singer. Author of *SWAMP!, Geek City Apocalypso, Urinals of Hell* and *Stumpfucker Cavalcade*. In 2003, Joe reprinted Lenore Kandel's banned erotic masterpiece *The Love Book*. Joe died in a Chinatown motel room in San Francisco, CA on July 26, 2017. A limited edition of previously unpublished poems, *Bozo Emergency*, was published by PachinkoPOPPress in 2018.

Kenneth Patchen (1911-1972) was an American poet and novelist. He experimented with different forms of writing incorporating painting, drawing, and jazz music into his works, which have been compared with those of William Blake and Walt Whitman. Along with his friend and peer Kenneth Rexroth, he was a central influence on the San Francisco Renaissance and the Beat Generation.

Stuart Z. Perkoff (1930-1974) Venice West poet, who, along with Tony Scibella and Frank T. Rios became a brotherhood that referred to themselves as "The Holy Three." Stuart is considered by many to be a spiritual, poetic center of Venice West. His books include *The Suicide Room* (Jargon Press, 1956) and his collected works *Voices of the Lady* (National Poetry Foundation, 1998).

D. A. Powell's books include *Chronic* (2009), *Useless Landscape or A Guide For Boys* (2012) and *Repast* (2014), all from Graywolf Press. A former Briggs-Copeland Lecturer at Harvard University, Powell currently teaches at University of San Francisco in the MFA Writing Program. His honors include fellowships from the NEA and the Guggenheim Foundation, the National Book Critics Circle Award in Poetry, the Shelley Memorial Award, the John Updike Award, and the California Book Award. His latest collection is *Atlas T* (2020) from Rescue Press.

Holly Prado (1938-2019), had thirteen books published, the last one being *Weather* (Cahuenga Press, 2019). Her previous books include poetry, prose-poetry, a novel, two novellas. She taught creative writing for many years, both privately and in the Master of Professional Writing Program at USC. She received a Certificate of Recognition from the City of Los Angeles for her work in the literary community. Also, Prado was the recipient of the 2016 George Drury Smith Award for Outstanding Achievement in Poetry.

Jerry the Priest has lived, taught and written in a plethora of glamorous and ignominious international locales. A vocalist since early childhood, his formal study of music began with his first trombone lesson in 1967. Essays, poems, stories, and illustrations have appeared in *Coagula Art Journal, La Quadra, The Nervous Breakdown, Bombay Gin*, etc. *Never a Dull Blundrr,* His anthological 'debut' LP is slated for release in 2022. Stay tuned.

Jeremy Radin is a writer, actor, teacher, and extremely amateur gardener. His poems have appeared (or are forthcoming) in *Ploughshares, The Colorado Review, Crazyhorse, Gulf Coast, The Journal*, and elsewhere. He is the author of two collections of poetry: *Slow Dance with Sasquatch* (Write Bloody Publishing, 2012) and *Dear Sal* (Not A Cult, 2017/2021). He was born and lives in Los Angeles. Follow him @germyradin

Kennon B. Raines started performing her poetry during the 80s in nightclubs & various venues from Atlanta, to NYC, London, Paris, Toronto, Montreal, Boston, Dallas, & San Francisco. In L.A. she's hosted monthly open mics at the Iguana Bookstore in NoHo, The Hole on 3rd St, & The Blue Nile on Fairfax. She's previously been published in LUMMOX #5 (2016); ONYX SPOKEN WORD, (Projector Press) and in the French Canadian art magazine, L'OEIL RECHARGEABLE. Producing & directing a theatrical evening of nude poetry, THE NAKED WORD, was especially gratifying for her & featured poets ranging in ages from 23 to 83 with live music.

A. Razor was first published as a street youth poet in the early 1980s punk zine era of Southern California, where he put his first chapbook out with Drew Blood Press, Ltd. in 1985 & published 11 more titles with them until 1996. He co-founded Punk Hostage Press with Iris Berry in 2012 & has edited other poets & writers for that PHP, as well as releasing 6 titles of his own poetry & prose, his most recent collection being entitled 'Puro Purismo' in 2020. He has done creative writing groups in jails & shelters since 2010 with the Words As Works program he helped found in that year.

Luivette Resto is an award-winning poet, a mother of 3 revolutionary humans, a Wonder Woman, and a middle school English teacher. She was born in Aguas Buenas, Puerto Rico but proudly raised in the Bronx. She is a CantoMundo and Macondo Fellow and a Pushcart Prize nominee. Her two books of poetry Unfinished Portrait and Ascension have been published by Tía Chucha Press. Her third poetry collection Living on Islands Not Found on Map, published by FlowerSong Press, is a finalist for the 2022 Juan Felipe Herrera Best Poetry Book Award at the International Latino Book Awards. She lives in the San Gabriel Valley in Los Angeles.

Kenneth Rexroth (1905-1982) was an American poet, translator, and critical essayist. He is regarded as a central figure in the San Francisco Renaissance, and paved the groundwork for the movement. Although he did not consider himself to be a Beat poet, and disliked the association, he was dubbed the "Father of the Beats" by *Time* magazine. Largely self-educated, Rexroth learned several languages and translated poems from Chinese, French, Spanish, and Japanese.

Kevin Ridgeway is the author of *Too Young to Know* (Stubborn Mule Press) and a dozen chapbooks of poetry including *Grandma Goes go Rehab* (Analog Submission Press, UK) and *In His Own Little World* (Between Shadows Press). His work has appeared in *Slipstream, Chiron Review, Cultural Daily, San Pedro River Review,* and *The American Journal of Poetry,* among others. His work has been nominated for the Pushcart Prize and Best of the Net. He lives and writes in Long Beach, CA.

Frank T. Rios (1936-2018), a street-smart kid from the Bronx, came to Venice in the late fifties, startling everyone with his black vision of holy pain. A survivor who has kept at it with a dignity and wisdom, inspiring those who think it just might be done: a life of poetry. Publications include his collected works, *Memoirs of a Street Poet* (Phony Lid, 2002). In 1992 he received the Joya C. Penobscot and the Tombstone Award for poetry in 1988.

Paul Corman-Roberts' second full length collection of poems *Bone Moon Palace* (Nomadic Press, 2021) was nominated for the 2021 CLMP Firecracker Award. An original founder and organizer of the Beast Crawl Lit Festival, he currently teaches workshops for the Older Writer's Lab in conjunction with the SF Public Library, the San Francisco Creative Writing Institute and the Oakland Unified School District. He sometimes fills in as a drummer for the U.S. Ghostal Service but mostly he is just exhausted.

Luis J. Rodriguez has 16 multi-genre books, including a bestselling memoir *Always Running*. He's founding editor of Tia Chucha Press and co-founder of Tia Chucha's Centro Cultural & Bookstore, based in the San Fernando Valley section of Los Angeles. His last poetry book was *Borrowed Bones* (Curbstone Books/Northwestern University Press, 2016). In 2020, Seven Stories Press released his books of essays *From Our Land to Our Land*. From 2014 to 2016, Luis served as Los Angeles' Poet Laureate.

Julie Rogers is a poet, author, writing coach, and the Director of TLC Transitional Life Care [www.tlcserves.org]. Her books include "Trading Fours" and "Sharing Breath", written with poet David Meltzer, and "Life on Earth" (Omerta), "House Of The Unexpected" (Wild Ocean Press), a CD, "Two-Tone Poetry & Jazz", recorded with David Meltzer and saxophonist Zan Stewart (Pureland Audio), and "Instructions for the Transitional State" (www.vimalatreasures.org), a Buddhist hospice manual.

California writer **Sylvia Ross** is the author of three historical novels: *Acts of Kindness, Acts of Contrition, East of the Great Valley,* and *Ilsa Rohe,* and she also published a book of short works, poems and drawings entitled: *ACORNS AND ABALONE.* She is also the author/illustrator of two culturally themed children's books: *Lion Singer* and *Blue Jay Girl.* She has work in many anthologies, and was one of four poets with Native connections who were invited to give a reading of their work at the MLA International Conference in San Diego in 2003.

Lee Rossi is a winner of both the Jack Grapes Poetry Prize and a runner-up for the Steve Kowit Prize. His latest book is *Darwin's Garden,* from Moon Tide Press. Individual poems have appeared in *The Southwest Review, Rattle, Spillway, The Chiron Review* and *The Southern Review.* He is a member of the Northern California Book Reviewers and a Contributing Editor to *Poetry Flash.*

CLS Sandoval, PhD is a Pushcart-nominated writer and communication professor with accolades in film, academia, and creative writing who speaks, signs, acts, publishes, sings, performs, writes, and paints. She has presented at academic conferences, published academic articles and books, poetry chapbooks, and three full-length literary collections: *God Bless Paul, Soup Stories: A Reconstructed Memoir,* and *Writing Our Love Story.* She enjoys life with her husband, daughter, and dog in Alhambra, CA.

Aram Saroyan is a poet, novelist, memoirist, playwright, and visual artist. He debuted as a writer with six poems and a review of Robert Creeley's novel The Island in the April 1964 issue of Poetry magazine. He became famous for his one-word poems, a form he developed during the early and mid-1960s, and which is often linked to concrete poetry. Saroyan's *Complete Minimal Poems* (2007) won the William Carlos Williams Award and his novel *The Romantic* (1988) was a Los Angeles Times Book Review Critic's Choice selection. Saroyan's honors and awards also include fellowships from the NEA.

Tony Scibella (1932-2003) was one of the true progenitors of the Venice West Beat scene in Southern California. Too poor to afford a middle name, he maintained a commitment to verse as poet and publisher for over 40 years, producing over 35 books and broadsides, under his own press: Black Ace. Tony's masterwork *The Kid in America / Black Ace Book 6* (Temple of Man, 1995), remains a seminal chronicle of beat culture in America.

Matt Sedillo has been described as the "best political poet in America" as well as "the poet laureate of the struggle" by academics, poets, and journalists alike. He has appeared on CSPAN, has been featured in the Los Angeles Times, spoken at Casa de las Americas in Havana, Cuba, and at over a hundred universities and colleges, including the University of Cambridge. He is the author of *Mowing Leaves of Grass* (Flower Song Press 2019) and *City on the Second Floor* (Flower Song Press 2022).

Kim Shuck is a silly protein. Shuck is the 7th San Francisco Poet Laureate Emerita. She is solo author of eight books, editor or co-editor of a further eight books, and has work in an unknown but large number of books by other people. Shuck holds an MFA in Textiles from San Francisco State University, she likes to fiddle with words and string.

Bucky Sinister is the author of four books of poetry (*King of the Roadkills*, *Whiskey & Robots*, *All Blacked Out* and *Nowhere to Go*, and *Time Bomb Snooze Alarm*), two self-help books (*Get Up* and *Still Standing*, and a science fiction novel (*Black Hole*). He ran poetry readings all through the '90s at The Chameleon in San Francisco. He lives in Los Angeles, where he samples as many taco trucks as possible while avoiding Dodger Dogs. He much prefers pie to cake but will still eat cake if you have some.

Gary Snyder is perhaps best known as a poet whose early work has been associated with the Beat Generation and the S.F. Renaissance. In 1975, he was awarded the Pulitzer Prize for his poetry collection, *Turtle Island*. Snyder is a prominent lecturer, environmental activist, and a recipient of the American Book Award. His writings reflect his devotion to nature and Buddhist spirituality. He has served as an academic at UC-Davis, and as a member of the California Arts Council.

Mike Sonksen aka **Mike the PoeT** is a 3rd-generation Southern Californian. Poet, professor, journalist, historian and tour-guide, his latest book *Letters to My City* was published by Writ Large Press. He's written for *KCET*, *Poets & Writers*, *Wax Poetics*, *PBS SoCal*, *LA Taco*, *LA Review of Books*, *LAist*, *Boom* and the *Academy of American Poets*. His poetry's been featured on Public Radio Stations KCRW, KPCC & KPFK & Spectrum News.

Jan Steckel's book *Like Flesh Covers Bone* won the 2019 Rainbow Awards for LGBT Poetry and Best Bisexual Book. Her poetry book *The Horizontal Poet* won a 2012 Lambda Literary Award for Bisexual Nonfiction. Her fiction chapbook *Mixing Tracks* and poetry chapbook *The Underwater Hospital* also won awards. She lives in Oakland, California.

Kimi Sugioka, is an educator and poet. She earned an MFA at Naropa University and has published two books of poetry; the newest of which is *Wile & Wing* (Manic D Press). As the Poet Laureate of Alameda, is engaging the community in a multi-cultural and intergenerational exploration of poetry and literature. Her work appears numerous anthologies. She believes that creating community through art is a revolutionary act.

Tate Swindell is a poet, painter, photographer and archivist who likes to talk with bees. Coeditor of the *Collected Poems of Bob Kaufman* (City Lights, 2019) and *On Valencia Street: Poems and Ephemera by Jack Micheline* (Lithic Press 2019). Tate runs the San Francisco based *Unrequited Records* which specializes in vinyl records from Beat Generation poets. Artist releases include Ronnie Burk, Gregory Corso, Herbert Huncke, Bob Kaufman, Jack Micheline and Harold Norse. Tate and his brother Todd were part of the early medical cannabis movement in San Francisco.

Mary TallMountain (1918-1994) was an Alaskan Athabaskan poet and storyteller. Adopted out from her tribe at an early age, much of her life and writing centered on reclaiming her lost roots and relations. She published widely and authored several collections, including *Light on the Tent Wall* (UCLA Press, 1990), and was featured in Bill Moyers' series, *Power of the Word*. The TallMountain Circle was founded to carry on her legacy of literary excellence and community leadership.

Chris Tannahill emigrated from Canada shortly after discovering Ginsberg, Corso and Paul Bowles in 1989. Fled to Boulder, Colorado in the mid-nineties and opened for the aforementioned Allen Ginsberg. Promptly returned to SoCal and was a member of the Hollywood and Orange County's slam teams. Featured at every possible venue south of Fresno, published *In Diabolic Gear* and *Inhuman* and *Out of Magic* with the Laguna Poets Press. Presently living about a quarter mile from Coachella Music Festival.

G. Murray Thomas used to attend poetry readings all over Southern California. Then he moved to upstate New York. We don't know what he does with his time now.

A. K. Toney is a Griot, writer and educator. He currently is a Literacy Coordinator, Artist teacher and owner of Reading Is Poetry. He is currently working on his first book and a current Spoken Word Jazz album entitled *Neo Griot and the Afrocentric Prince*. Toney embodies his Oral Tradition Music as labeled by chronicling his life as a poet in the Leimert Park Village area in Los Angeles, CA.

Kelly Grace Thomas is an ocean-obsessed Aries from Jersey. She is a poet, editor, and educator. Kelly is the winner of the 2020 Jane Underwood Poetry Prize and 2017 Neil Postman Award for Metaphor from *Rattle*. Her first full-length collection, *Boat Burned*, released with YesYes Books in January 2020. Kelly's poems have appeared: *Best New Poets 2019, Los Angeles Review, Muzzle* and more. Kelly is the Director of Education for Get Lit. www.kellygracethomas.com

Lynne Thompson is the 2021-22 Poet Laureate for the City of Los Angeles. Thompson is the author of three collections of poetry, most recently, *Fretwork*, winner of the Marsh Hawk Poetry Prize. The recipient of multiple awards, her recent work appears or is forthcoming in *New York Quarterly, Black Warrior Review, Massachusetts Review* and 2020 *Best American Poetry*. Thompson sits on the Boards of Cave Canem and the Los Angeles Review of Books. www.lynnethompson.us

David L. Ulin is the author or editor of many books, including *Sidewalking: Coming to Terms with Los Angeles*, which was shortlisted for the PEN/Diamonstein-Spielvogel Award for the Art of the Essay. He is a Professor of English at the University of Southern California, where he edits the journal *Air/Light*.

Amy Uyematsu is a sansei poet and teacher from Los Angeles. She has five published collections - the most recent being *Basic Vocabulary* in 2016. Her sixth book, *That Blue Trickster Time*, is forthcoming in 2022. Her first poetry collection, *30 Miles from J-Town*, won the 1992 Nicholas Roerich Poetry Prize. Active in Asian American Studies when it first emerged in the late 60s, she was co-editor of the widely used UCLA anthology, *Roots: An Asian American Reader*.

Fred Voss has been a machinist for 43 years. He has published 3 books of poetry with Bloodaxe Books (U.K.). The latest of them, *Hammers and Hearts of the Gods*, was selected a Book of the Year 2009 by the Morning Star (London). He won the Joe Hill Labor Poetry award in 2016. His novel, *Making America Strong*, a satire on the making of nuclear bombers, is available from Amazon.

Since 1950 **Joan Jobe Smith Voss's** award-winning poetry has appeared internationally in 100s of publications. She is the founding editor of PEARL lit journal and Bukowski Review. In her 70s, Joan published *Charles Bukowski: EPIC GLOTTIS: His Art & His Women (& me)*, a literary memoir of her decade friendship w/Charles Bukowski (Silver Birch Press 2012); *Tales of An Ancient Go-Go Girl*, (MarJo Books, 2015); *Moonglow a Go-Go*, (New York Quarterly 2017) and *Made in the Shade* (Tangerine Press, 2020).

Ken Wainio (1952-2006), considered to be one of America's finest surrealist writers, was a poet and novelist from northern California who spent most of his life in San Francisco. He began to write at 15, having been influenced by the French poets Rimbaud, Lautremont, and Nerval. During his time in S.F., he was influenced by poets such as Philip Lamantia, Harold Norse, and Neeli Cherkovski. Wainio is the author of such books as *Letters from Al Kemi*, *Two Lives, Crossroads of the Other*, and *STARFUCK* (a novel published on computer disk by New Native Press).

Scott Wannberg (1953-2011) Scott loved cats, dogs, movies, writing spontaneous poems for strangers and riding shotgun in the 1959 Cadillac as a Carma Bum. Scott received his Masters in Creative Writing from San Francisco State University in 1977. His titles include *Mr. Mumps* (Ouija Madness, 1982), *The Electric Yes Indeed* (Shelf Life Press, 1989), *Nomads of Oblivion* (Lummox Press, 2000) and most recently *The Official Language of Yes!* (Perceval Press, 2015).

LA native, **Pam Ward** just released her poetry book BETWEEN GOOD MEN & NO MAN AT ALL (World Stage Press). She's published two novels, WANT SOME GET SOME, and BAD GIRLS BURN SLOW (Kensington). A UCLA graduate, recipient of a California Arts Council Fellow, a Pushcart Poetry Nominee, Ward has published in *Chiron, Calyx, Voices of Leimert Park* and the *LA Times*. She's currently working on a novel about her aunt's dalliance in the Black Dahlia Murder. www.pamwardwriter.com.

Charles Harper Webb's latest collection of poems, *Sidebend World*, was published by the University of Pittsburgh Press in 2018. Recipient of grants from the Whiting and Guggenheim foundations, Webb teaches Creative Writing at California State University, Long Beach. His novel *Ursula Lake* was published by Red Hen Press in 2022.

Lew Welch's (1926-1971) poetry explores themes of nature, pop culture, and spiritual practice. He was often grouped with the Beat poets, and described as "a postmodern Walt Whitman." Welch published several collections of poetry including *Wobbly Rock* (1960) and *Hermit Poems* (1965). His prose includes *How I Work as a Poet* (1973) and *How I Read Gertrude Stein* (1996, published posthumously). His 1973 collection, *Ring of Bone: Collected Poems*, was expanded by poet Gary Snyder in 2012, with a new introduction.

Saul White (1932-2003), Venice West abstract expressionist and jazz poet. Saul was born in New York, moving to Los Angeles in 1945. After serving during the Korean War, Saul attended Otis Art Institute on a fellowship. In the mid 1950s he rented a storefront in Venice on Ocean Avenue which became a gathering place for artists Wallace Berman, Edward Kienholz and John Altoon. In 1957 Saul was part of a series of readings with Kenneth Patchen and Kenneth Rexroth, the poets accompanied by Shorty Rogers' jazz band.

Aruni Wijesinghe is a project manager, ESL teacher, occasional sous chef and erstwhile belly dance instructor. She holds a BA in English, an AA in dance, and a certification in TESOL. A Pushcart Prize-nominated poet, her work has been published in journals and anthologies both nationally and internationally, with solo poetry collections forthcoming in 2022. She lives a quiet life in Orange County, California with her husband Jeff and their cats Jack and Josie.

Conney D. Williams is a poet, actor, community activist, and performance artist with three collections of poetry *"Leaves of Spilled Spirit from an Untamed Poet (2002)"* and "Blues Red Soul Falsetto (2012); his new collection *"the distance of observation"* was released August 2021 on World Stage Press. He also has two critically acclaimed poetry CDs: *River&Moan* and *Unsettled Water*.

Jessica M. Wilson is a Chicana Beat Poet from East Los Angeles, California. She holds an MFA in Writing from Otis College of Art & Design, & BA in Creative Writing & Art History from the University of California Riverside. Jessica founded the Los Angeles Poet Society, she's a 3rd Generation Beatnik, & an International Poet. Stay in touch: www.jessicamwilson.com

A. D. Winans is an award winning native San Francisco poet, writer, and publishere. He published Second Coming Mag/Press from 1972-89. Awards include a PEN National Josephine Miles Award for literary excellence, a PEN Oakland Lifetime Achievement Award, and a Kathy Acker award in poetry and publishing.

CeciliaWoloch is the author of six collections of poems and a novel, as well as essays and reviews. Her honors include fellowships from the National Endowment for the Arts, the California Arts Council, CEC/Arts Link International and the Center for International Theatre Development; her work has also received a Pushcart Prize and been included in the *Best American Poetry* Series. Based in Los Angeles, she is currently a Fulbright fellow at the University of Rzeszów in southeastern Poland.

Terry Wolverton is author of eleven books of poetry, fiction, and creative nonfiction, including *Embers*, a novel in poems, and *Insurgent Muse: art and life at the Woman's Building*, a memoir. Terry has received a COLA Fellowship from the City of Los Angeles and a Fellowship in Poetry from the California Arts Council, among other honors. She is the founder of Writers At Work, a creative writing studio in Los Angeles, and Affiliate Faculty in the MFA Writing Program at Antioch University Los Angeles. www.terrywolverton.net

Daniel Yaryan is the poet-author of the illustrated volume *Sorcerers: Through Dimensions Infinite*, a collaboration with fantasy artist Fitz. "It is the first full volume of cosmic pulp poetry," says Los Angeles poet/writer Nelson Gary, who also calls the book "ingenious." Yaryan is the founder of the Mystic Boxing Commission, curator of the Kamstra Sparring Archive and an event organizer throughout California. He is editor of the upcoming *Sparring With Beatnik Ghosts Omnibus*. His books are available at www.sparringartists.com.

Mariano Zaro is the author of six books of poetry, most recently *Decoding Sparrows* (What Books Press), finalist of the Housatonic Book Award, and *Padre Tierra* (Olifante). His poems and short stories have been published in anthologies and literary journals in Spain, Mexico and United States. He has translated American poets Philomene Long, Tony Barnstone and Sholeh Wolpé. He is a professor of Spanish at Rio Hondo Community College (Whittier, CA). Website: www.marianozaro.com

ACKNOWLEDGEMENTS

Moon Tide Press and the poets in this anthology are grateful to the following estates, and the publications where these poems have previously appeared, sometimes in a different form:

Terry Adams - "Breath" - *Adam's Ribs*, Off The Grid Press, 2008, and *The Sun*, June 1994

Kim Addonizio - "Creased Map of the Underworld" - *My Black Angel: Blues Poems and Portraits*, Stephen F. Austin University Press

Ellen Bass - "The Small Country" - *Indigo* (Copper Canyon Press, 2020)

Charles Bukowski - "the tragedy of the leaves" – permission granted by Ecco/Harper Collins

Carolyn Cassady - "Poetic Portraits" from *Poetic Portrait, Carolyn Cassady Revealed in Poetry and Prose*. Prose by Cathy Cassady / Poetry by Carolyn Cassady

Neal Cassady - "Third Anniversary Poem from Neal to Carolyn" – opening paragraph by Carolyn Cassady, beginning of Chapter 26, *Off the Road: My Years with Cassady, Kerouac and Ginsberg* by Carolyn Cassady. Copyright Estate of Neal & Carolyn Cassady

Wanda Coleman - "O Soul Concealed Below" – *The World Falls Away*, University of Pittsburgh Press, 2011

Larry Colker – "Crossing Over" (Exhibit #204) appears in *Amnesia and Wings* (Tebot Bach, 2013)

Peter Coyote - "Flags" – *Tongue of a Crow*, Four Way Books, 2021

Peggy Dobreer - "A Kara:U Kara:M Kara:Iti" – Slow Lightning

Kim Dower - "Doing Nothing" - *James Dickey Review*, Fall, 2021

Elisabeth Adwin Edwards - "Ode to Iron" – *SWWIM*

Alexis Rhone Fancher - "When I asked him to turn me on he said:" – *The American Journal of Poetry*, 2017. Made into a broadside by Phantom Bill Stickers & plastered all over New Zealand, 2021

Rich Ferguson - "When Called in For Questioning" – *Everything Is Radiant Between the Hates*, Moon Tide Press

francEyE - "Call" – first published in *Call* (Rose of Sharon Press). Reprinted by permission of Marina Bukowski

Frank X. Gaspar – "Can't You Hear the Wind Howl" - *Night of a Thousand Blossoms*, Alice James Books

Robert Hass - "Dancing" - *Bullets into Bells: Poets and Citizens Respond to Gun Violence*. Copyright © 2017 by Robert Hass. Reprinted by permission of Robert Hass

Jack Hirschman - "Path" - first published in *Fists on Fire* (Sore Dove Press, 2003) copyright Agneta Falk Hirschman

Bob Kaufman - "Would You Wear My Eyes?" – Reprinted with permission of the estate of Bob Kaufman

Douglas Kearney – "Headnote to a Done Poem" - *Buck Studies* (Fence Books, 2016)

Joanne Kyger - "Destruction" - from *About Now: Collected Poems*

La Loca – "You Should Only Give Head to Guys You Really Like" - *Adventures on the Isle of Adolesence*, City Lights Books, 1989

Philip Lamantia - "Poem for André Breton" - Reprinted by permission of Nancy J. Peters and the Estate of Philip Lamantia, 1997

Philip Levine - "They Feed They Lion" – *They Feed They Lion and the Names of the Lost: Poems* (Penguin Random House: 1968, 2969, 1970, 1971, 1972)

Ellaraine Lockie - "Then and Now" - *San Gabriel Valley Poetry Quarterly*

Philomene Long – "Mirrors are Sleeping Winds" – Reprinted by permission of Pegarty Long

Suzanne Lummis – "He Really" - *The Normal School*, Spring 2019—CSU Fresno

Lewis MacAdams - "The Voice of the River" - *THE RIVER: BOOKS ONE, TWO & THREE* (Blue Press, 2007)

Phoebe MacAdams - "Even Birds Are Complicated" - *Touching Stone*, Cahuenga Press, 2012

William J. Margolis - "A (PROSE)POEM STRICTLY FOR THE LOCAL SCENE, LIKE, MAYBE IT'S AN OPEN LETTER TO HERBERT Q. CAEN" – *Temple of Man*

Clint Margrave - "A Supermarket in California" - *Another Chicago Magazine*

David Meltzer – "RE: 2016" – Reprinted by permission of Julie Rogers and the Estate of David Meltzer

Jack Micheline - "I AM A POET" – Reprinted with permission of the Jack Micheline estate

mike m mollett - "dystopian revenge for the new year hell of it" – *Raw Cuts, a poetic manifesto*

Eric Morago - "Smolder" appears in *Feasting in Sky* (Paper Plane Pilots, 2016)

Jim Morrison – "Dry Water" - *The Los Angeles Image, 1969, Vol. 1, Number 12, October 13-16*

Harold Norse - "North Beach" – *In the hub of the fiery force: collected poems of Harold Norse 1934-2003* (Bancroft Library / UC Regents)

Dion O'Reilly - "Peacock" – *Catamaran*

Joe Pachinko - "God is an Asshole" - Reprinted by permission of the Estate of Joe Pachinko

D. A. Powell – *"Don't Touch My Junk"* – Four Way Review

Holly Prado - "For Poets In Autumn" – *Specific Mysteries*, Cahuenga Press, 1990

Kenneth Rexroth - "Fox" - *A Bestiary for daughters Mariana & Katherine*

Kevin Ridgeway - "Social Distance" - *Misfit Magazine*

Frank T. Rios – "Invocation" – *Temple of Man*

Aram Saroyan - "Life is a Dream" - *Day and Night: Bolinas Poems* (Black Sparrow Press, 1998) By permission of Aram Saroyan

Tony Scibella – "Spring Swing" - *Temple of Man*

Gary Snyder – "Night Songs of the Los Angeles Basin" – *Danger on Peaks*, Counterpoint Press, 2004

Mary Tallmountain - "Coyote in the Mission" - *Listen to the Night: Poems for the Animals Spirits of Mother Earth*, Freedom Voices, 1995

G. Murray Thomas – "Death to the Real World" appears in Cows on the Freeway (Writers Club Press, 2000)

David Ulin - *"Our Son Comes Over"* was originally published in Alta Journal, Issue 18, Winter 2022

Amy Uyematsu - "This Is" - *Rigorous*, Volume 15, Issue 2, 2021

Yvonne de la Vega - "I Write and I Fuck" – *Tomorrow, Yvonne: Poetry & Prose for Suicidal Egotists*, Punk Hostage Press, 2012

Fred Voss - "The Earth and the Stars In the Palm of My Hand" - *Culture Matters*, Manifesto Press, U.K.

Scott Wannberg – "The Dancer Steps Forward" – First published in *Tomorrow is Another Song* (Perceval Press), copyright Estate of Scott Wannberg

Lew Welch - "Song of the Turkey Buzzard" – *Ring of Bone: Collected Poems 1950-1971*, City Lights Books

Saul White – "The Funny Style Cat" – *Temple of Man*

Cecilia Woloch - "For the Birds: A Charm of Goldfinches" - *Earth* (Two Sylvias Press, 2015)

Terry Wolverton – "Transient" - *Van Gogh's Ear*, Volume 7, edited by Felice Picano, French Connection Press, Paris, France. 2010

THANKS AND MORE THANKS

My fellow editors and I are extremely grateful to the following people for their love, generosity, knowledge and support helping to make this anthology a reality:

Tosh Berman, Kelly Besser, Ianthe Brautigan, Marina Bukowski, John Cassady, Jami Cassady Ratto, Cathy Cassady Silvia, Frederick T. Courtright, Thomas Rain Crowe, Soheyl Dahi, Tristin Dillon, Rachel DiPaola, John Dorsey, Michael C Ford, Amelie Frank, Gina Gamma, Molly Haigh, Brian Hassett, Robert Parker Kaufman, Debbie Tosun Kilday, Pegarty Long, Phoebe MacAdams, George & Sharon Mitchell, Richard Modiano, Anne Morrison, Eileen L. O'Malley, Lorraine Perrotta, Nancy J. Peters, Paul Richmond, Tate Swindell, Todd Swindell, Kennon B. Raines, Christopher Robin, , Julie Rogers, Sheree Rose, Vince Silvaer, Blaise Smith, Gary Snyder, V. Vale.

Special thanks to all the poets whose work is showcased in this anthology. Your collective voices have made this collection far mightier than we editors could have ever imagined.

Huge and heartfelt gratitude to Kathleen Florence. Thank you for planting the poetry seed that grew this book into what it is today.

Special thanks to the estates of poets no longer with us. We're incredibly honored that you've allowed us to showcase the work of such esteemed poets.

Lastly, we offer endless gratitude and appreciation to the poets in this book who are no longer with us. Your literary inspirations continue to reverberate through our hearts and minds, and the poems we write daily.

Patrons

Moon Tide Press would like to thank the following people for their support in helping publish the finest poetry from the Southern California region. To sign up as a patron, visit www.moontidepress.com or send an email to publisher@moontidepress.com.

Anonymous
Robin Axworthy
Conner Brenner
Nicole Connolly
Bill Cushing
Susan Davis
Kristen Baum DeBeasi
Peggy Dobreer
Kate Gale
Dennis Gowans
Alexis Rhone Fancher
Hanalena Fennel
Half Off Books & Brad T. Cox
Donna Hilbert
Jim & Vicky Hoggatt
Michael Kramer
Ron Koertge & Bianca Richards
Gary Jacobelly
Ray & Christi Lacoste
Jeffery Lewis
Zachary & Tammy Locklin
Lincoln McElwee
David McIntire
José Enrique Medina
Michael Miller & Rachanee Srisavasdi
Michelle & Robert Miller
Ronny & Richard Morago
Terri Niccum
Andrew November
Jeremy Ra
Luke & Mia Salazar
Jennifer Smith
Roger Sponder
Andrew Turner
Rex Wilder
Mariano Zaro
Wes Bryan Zwick

Also Available from Moon Tide Press

When There Are Nine: Poems Celebrating the Life and Achievements of Ruth Bader Ginsburg (2022)
The Knife Thrower's Daughter, Terri Niccum (2022)
2 Rever Place, Aruni Wijesinghe (2022)
Here Go the Knives, Kelsey Bryan-Zwick (2022)
Trumpets in the Sky, Jerry Garcia (2022)
Threnody, Donna Hilbert (2022)
A Burning Lake of Paper Suns, Ellen Webre (2021)
Instructions for an Animal Body, Kelly Gray (2021)
Head *V* Heart: New & Selected Poems, Rob Sturma (2021)
Sh!t Men Say to Me: A Poetry Anthology in Response to Toxic Masculinity (2021)
Flower Grand First, Gustavo Hernandez (2021)
Everything is Radiant Between the Hates, Rich Ferguson (2020)
When the Pain Starts: Poetry as Sequential Art, Alan Passman (2020)
This Place Could Be Haunted If I Didn't Believe in Love, Lincoln McElwee (2020)
Impossible Thirst, Kathryn de Lancellotti (2020)
Lullabies for End Times, Jennifer Bradpiece (2020)
Crabgrass World, Robin Axworthy (2020)
Contortionist Tongue, Dania Ayah Alkhouli (2020)
The only thing that makes sense is to grow, Scott Ferry (2020)
Dead Letter Box, Terri Niccum (2019)
Tea and Subtitles: Selected Poems 1999-2019, Michael Miller (2019)
At the Table of the Unknown, Alexandra Umlas (2019)
The Book of Rabbits, Vince Trimboli (2019)
Everything I Write Is a Love Song to the World, David McIntire (2019)
Letters to the Leader, HanaLena Fennel (2019)
Darwin's Garden, Lee Rossi (2019)
Dark Ink: A Poetry Anthology Inspired by Horror (2018)
Drop and Dazzle, Peggy Dobreer (2018)
Junkie Wife, Alexis Rhone Fancher (2018)
The Moon, My Lover, My Mother, & the Dog, Daniel McGinn (2018)
Lullaby of Teeth: An Anthology of Southern California Poetry (2017)
Angels in Seven, Michael Miller (2016)
A Likely Story, Robbi Nester (2014)
Embers on the Stairs, Ruth Bavetta (2014)
The Green of Sunset, John Brantingham (2013)

The Savagery of Bone, Timothy Matthew Perez (2013)
The Silence of Doorways, Sharon Venezio (2013)
Cosmos: An Anthology of Southern California Poetry (2012)
Straws and Shadows, Irena Praitis (2012)
In the Lake of Your Bones, Peggy Dobreer (2012)
I Was Building Up to Something, Susan Davis (2011)
Hopeless Cases, Michael Kramer (2011)
One World, Gail Newman (2011)
What We Ache For, Eric Morago (2010)
Now and Then, Lee Mallory (2009)
Pop Art: An Anthology of Southern California Poetry (2009)
In the Heaven of Never Before, Carine Topal (2008)
A Wild Region, Kate Buckley (2008)
Carving in Bone: An Anthology of Orange County Poetry (2007)
Kindness from a Dark God, Ben Trigg (2007)
A Thin Strand of Lights, Ricki Mandeville (2006)
Sleepyhead Assassins, Mindy Nettifee (2006)
Tide Pools: An Anthology of Orange County Poetry (2006)
Lost American Nights: Lyrics & Poems, Michael Ubaldini (2006)

www.ingramcontent.com/pod-product-compliance
Lightning Source LLC
LaVergne TN
LVHW091826230125
802001LV00003B/210